Praise for Handcuffs to Broken Chains

"In the New Testament, Paul says that 'the gospel is the power of God unto salvation.' I belie of my being, and one of the greatest is the life-changing story of Cody changed by knowing him, and yours this powerful story of God's amazing

Vance Pitman
Senior Pastor, Hope Church

"Hurt people hurt people, but healthy people heal people. Cody's story is about a hurt man who found the one true healer and began a ministry of healing the hurt."

Tim Harlow
Senior Pastor, Parkview Christian Church

"Cody Huff is the real deal. He's full of life and faith and his hope overflows in these pages. Handcuffs to Broken Chains will ignite your faith and empower you to step out and pursue the God who loves you. Freedom is only a step of faith away and Cody illustrates how we can all take that step and become the people God desires for us to become."

Jud Wilhite
*Author of **Pursued***
Senior Pastor, Central Christian Church

"Handcuffs to Broken Chains is a very raw and compelling journey that demonstrates God's grace. Amazing grace is experienced in Cody's personal journey. It continues today in Cody's ministry of hope to the homeless. I believe God will say to Cody in heaven, 'Job well done, my loyal and faithful servant.'"

Jim Jackson
Leadership Coach, JimJacksonLive.com

HANDCUFFS
to
BROKEN CHAINS

From Abused, Addicted and Homeless - to Abundance

Cody Huff

Foreword by
Lee Strobel

Editing and writing assistance from Heidi Wallenborn

Cover design: Daria Lacy

Special quantity discounts may be available for this title. For bulk purchase questions go to www.VegasBrokenChains.org

Publisher Disclaimer

Published in the United States of America
by Colossus Publishing

ISBN: 978-1-941256-00-8

Interview, transcription, and writing assistance provided by **BookByInterview.com**

Colossus Publishing is a publisher of non-fiction books authored by thought leaders and entrepreneurs that wish to share their experience, stories, passion, and ideas with the world. If you have a book idea that you would like us to consider for publishing, please request an Info-Pack at www.ColossusPublishing.com

Table of Contents

PART 1

PART 2

ACKNOWLEDGEMENTS

I would like, first, to acknowledge my Lord and Savior, Jesus Christ, who transformed me from a homeless drug addict into the person that I am today. I now have a loving relationship with the Father. He loves His kids so very much. I am so blessed to be a part of His Kingdom activity on this earth. I pray that this book touches hearts for His Kingdom!

Next I would like to thank my lovely wife, Heather, for the unconditional love she has shown me over the last 10 years. Heather has worked tirelessly to make Broken Chains a success. Heather has been the Proverbs 31 wife to me. I am forever grateful to Heather for her love, encouragement and heart for the less fortunate of our city.

I would like to thank Kenny and Jean Atcheson for taking on the financial and creative responsibility, without which this book would never have been written. I would like to thank Heidi Wallenborn for her diligence, dedication, hard work, and for bringing this book to life.

I would also like to thank Peter Blue of Evident Productions, who designed and donated our wonderful new website "VegasBrokenChains.org" This website has attracted people from all over the United States to volunteer, serve and donate to the ministry.

I would like to thank all of our sponsors and volunteers, and the Hope Church family who continually assist with all the happenings at Broken Chains. And a special thanks to all my mentors, accountability partners, especially Pastor Vance Pitman for pouring into my development and taking me into the deeper things of God's word.

Also, many thanks to Lee Strobel, who put my testimony in his latest book "The Case for Grace," had me as a guest at Woodlands Church in Texas, and wrote the Foreword for this book. Lee, I am proud to call you my friend and brother.

FOREWORD

All right, I'll admit it: I'm an addict. I can't help it – I'm a fanatic when it comes to stories about how God transforms lives.

I've watched a vicious street gang leader become the compassionate pastor of an inner city church. I've seen a death-row killer released from prison because Jesus had so thoroughly transformed him. I've observed a God-hater morph into an evangelist. I've witnessed a Ku Klux Klan terrorist become the loving pastor of a multi-racial congregation.

I'm friends with a convicted felon, once depleted of all hope at one of America's toughest prisons, who was given purpose by God – a new vision and ministry that is now helping thousands of churches tell others about Jesus. I've watched atheists become missionaries, once-wayward kids become worship leaders, narcissists become selfless servants, and ordinary folks who thought they had it all until they discovered there's nothing more important than Christ.

And, of course, I've seen up close how God can save "a wretch like me," rescuing my life, my marriage, and my family with his amazing grace.

I can't get enough of it. These kinds of stories give hope that nobody is beyond redemption and transformation.

Not even my friend Cody Huff.

You'll read Cody's story in the pages to come, but let me prepare you: you will be astounded, encouraged, and inspired by how God showered his grace on this man who had spent his entire life running away from Him.

Cody's spiritual journey is among the most colorful and compelling I've ever encountered. In fact, he was one of the unlikeliest candidates for following Christ that I've ever met. When he first unpacked for me the details of his once wayward life, I was overwhelmed by how God has absolutely revolutionized his soul, turned his priorities upside down, and given him a mission in life that really matters.

Now I'm privileged to be his friend and spiritual brother.

Are you intrigued? Well, read on – and be ready by the end of the book to breathe a prayer of gratitude to the God who's still very much in the life transformation business.

– Lee Strobel
Author, *The Case for Christ* and *The Case for Grace*

PREFACE

The end of me

I was starving. I hadn't eaten in three days.

At age 51, I was a homeless drug addict in Las Vegas. It was July 2003; I'd been living on the streets there for about a year.

My pattern was that I would do drugs – mostly smoke crack — for two or three days and not feed myself, then go back to a dirt field behind the police station at night to sleep in a little hole I had carved out of a purple-flowered oleander bush.

Early one morning I woke up about three o'clock. Even at that hour, the dry desert heat lingered. It was still too warm, I was covered in flies, and I was famished. The place I called home was on Fremont Street near hotels that doubled as crack houses. I looked across the field and noticed a dumpster behind Odyssey Pizza. I thought, *Wow, I am so hungry.* I had no idea that hunger could hurt so bad.

So I carefully stood up. Walking on skinny, shaky legs and bent over with hunger, I made my way across the street. The dumpster stank. Flies hovered over scraps of food in the hot metal bin. Skinny, scrounging cats and dogs scurried out of my way. There were boxes in there with scraps of pizza – so many people don't eat the crust. I leaned in and dug around the garbage. I found more; there were whole chicken wings and a few where somebody had taken a bite. I grabbed what I could find and chowed into that stuff.

I was ravenous. I didn't care. There was a lot of food in the dumpster that night; my stomach was full for the first time in a long time.

As I stood there wiping grease and crumbs from my scraggly, dirty beard, it hit me — what I had just done. As far as I was concerned at that moment, it was the worst thing I'd ever done in my life; and in all of my years I had done some really bad things.

In all of the times and places that I'd been nearly destitute, I had never eaten out of a garbage can - never in my life. I hadn't even thought about getting food poisoning. All I cared about was getting food into my stomach.

When you're homeless, your self-respect and dignity take a nosedive from the moment that you sleep on the street for the first time. But just then, when I'd had my fill from a dumpster, it really hit me — my dignity had disintegrated like wet cardboard. I was in so much pain from hunger that all I could think about was getting rid of it.

There was nothing left of me. If I'd had a gun at that moment, I would have put it in my mouth and pulled the trigger.

I crumbled inside and sank to my knees in the filthy alley. My life has come to this. Now I'm scrounging and eating out of garbage cans like a rat. I was overcome by the stark reality that I was homeless and that I was a drug addict.

And I was mad. I hated people, I hated God, I hated everything. I hated me; I hated the situation I was in. And there was no way out.

I cried like a baby for nearly an hour. I didn't know that tears could make a mud puddle. I cried and I cried, because my heart was so broken and I didn't have any way to become – and I knew that I would never be – a normal person again. I knew that my life was headed toward destruction.

I didn't have any hope. I didn't have any peace.

I was crushed under the unbearable weight that crashed down on me.

This was the beginning of the end – of the old me.

Part 1

CHAPTER 1

Growing Up Years

As far back as I can remember I knew that I wasn't wanted. My mother and others told me so – especially my mother. I was unloved. It seemed like everything I did was wrong.

My father was 19-years-old when he got my 14-year-old mother pregnant. I have never seen my father. I talked to him once when I was 25. I called after extensive investigation to find him and explained that I was his son. When I asked if he ever wondered what happened to me or whatever had become of me, his answer was, "No, not really."

In the 1950s, especially in a little town like Klamath Falls, Oregon, it was a disgrace to the family when a young, unmarried girl got pregnant. Although my mom married my father they never lived together. It was a shotgun wedding

– literally. Her dad, my grandfather, went to my dad and said, "Either marry my daughter because you're the one who knocked her up, or I'm going to get my shotgun." My grandfather was a cop. So my father married my mother to give me a name and so she could get some kind of child support. Then they got a divorce.

I was born June 7, 1951 in Klamath Falls. Mom's family immediately shipped her off to Marysville, California with me to where her older brother Don lived. And, well, I really don't know how to put this other than I had a lot of uncles, okay? I had a *lot* of uncles. Before I was five-years-old I would go into my mom's room in the morning two or three times a week and find that I had another uncle. That was my mom's profession at that time. She was a "waitress" and drove a brand-new Cadillac.

This pain of being unwanted and unloved developed more throughout my childhood — I saw regular families with children. I saw my friends being loved by their parents and taken places and bought things. As young as five-years-old I felt worthless. Even at that age my mom told me that I would never amount to anything, I would never do anything, and that everything I would do I would quit.

Beatings and mental abuse were mostly because I was not living up to her expectations. I remember a whipping with a belt that left me bleeding from my neck to down below my knees when I was not much older than a toddler. If the laws we have today about child abuse were in place then, my mother would have been arrested and put in prison.

My mother often told me, "I wish I never would have had you," "You've been nothing but a problem," "If I didn't have you, I could be doing more important things with my life." All of those negative comments formed how I thought about myself. It is true what the Bible says, "As man thinks, so he is."

When I was four or five-years-old, Mom got married again and had a baby boy with her husband. It turned out that this man wasn't honest about his profession; he said that he was a businessman. Well, it turned out he was a bank robber. We lived in Roseville, California at the time, and the police showed up at our door. They told her that they had arrested her husband for bank robbery. We never heard from him again. I didn't mind him too much, because he taught me how to fish which came in handy much later in my life.

So, now my mom was single with two kids and she kept up her "waitressing" business for income. Both of us boys were excessively abused. Her excuse was always that we didn't live up to her expectations. The funny thing is that from when I began school up until I started smoking pot at age 13, I got really good grades.

However, there was a hero during part of my childhood. From around six-years-old until I turned 13, my uncle Glen who was married to my mother's sister lived in Klamath Falls. He knew about the abuse and did everything that he could to help me. Every once in a while Uncle Glen would show up at my mother's door after we moved to Marysville and say, "You pack that kid's clothes; he is going with me."

Uncle Glen was my superhero. The few times that I went to live with him I knew that he was gonna take care of me and I was gonna be okay and I wasn't gonna be beaten. He taught me how to waterski, work on cars and ride motorcycles. When he took me out on the bike, he let me drive it one mile up the road and one mile back to his house.

It was wonderful living with him. I wanted to stay forever. He had two daughters and a son, and whenever I was there I was a part of one big happy family. I never felt that I was just a nephew — I wasn't treated as anything other than a son. He showed me what a real man should be.

But there always came a point – I still don't know the dynamics of it – that I would have to go back home. And when I went back home I paid for it. The beatings increased, especially when Mom found out that I told my aunt and uncle what she did to me.

I don't know the underlying forces of why I had to go back to my mom. I never understood why I had to go back.

CHAPTER 2

Early Drug Years

I was introduced to marijuana in 1963 when I was 13 and living in Marysville, about 40 miles north of Sacramento. It made me feel good about myself. Those things that my mother made me believe about my personality and appearance were pushed into oblivion.

When I was introduced to marijuana I found a group of friends that I could hang out with who cared about me. I got high with them and they replaced my family.

Like many drug addicts, I started using marijuana maybe once a week. Then it turned into twice a week, then every day. After a while I didn't want to have anything to do with school or anything else.

Also at 13, I started running away to the Haight-Ashbury district in San Francisco to live with hippies for extended periods of time. There were about 15 of us crammed into an old Victorian house. I thumbed the 124 miles from Marysville to The City. In the 1960s, running away from home and not going to school was a charge called "Out of Control."

I really was spiraling out of control; I was arrested for being "Out of Control" four times. When I ran away the first few times, my mom reported me missing so the police put out a BOLO – Be On the Look Out. The first time I ran away, I was gone for four months. After that, they knew where to find me. The police hauled me back to Marysville and put me in juvenile hall. My first time I did 30 days. The second time was for 90 days, and after the third time when I did six months my mom told them to keep me. After they let me out I ran away again, was caught, and did one year.

Every time they let me out I was put on probation and told that I had to go back to school or I'd take a trip back to juvie. I guess you can figure out what I did.

Funny thing is, I never got busted for the only real crime that I had committed up to that point which was using and selling marijuana.

After I started doing pot and running away, I didn't see Uncle Glen anymore. I stayed away on purpose because I knew he loved me and I didn't want to disappoint him.

You know, when I ran from home I didn't really think about breaking the law. All I thought about was that I wanted to get away from my mother. I was abused, mistreated and neglected. No one cared about *that* part – what *she* did to *me*. For whatever reason, living with Uncle Glen wasn't an option anymore, and I wanted to live my life without fear.

So I took matters into my own hands. There was freedom in being a runaway, especially during the '60s in Haight-Ashbury. It meant that I could do anything that I wanted whenever I wanted.

When I scampered off to The City, I met people who introduced me to heavy-duty drugs: LSD, peyote, cocaine, speed. Those took me away from the reality of the pain in my heart. Yet again I was part of a new family who wanted freedom too. At the ripe old age of 13, I felt like, *You know what? Just forget all that bad stuff that happened to you — your life is moving forward, you're not going to think about the past.* And I never did. I escaped reality.

In those days I was high a lot but I wasn't an addict. I didn't start using addictive drugs regularly until many years later. But I did a lot of magic mushrooms and once or twice a week I'd trip on LSD if my friends and I were going to concerts. That stuff took me far away from reality. It was like being in an animated world – I walked down the street and houses took on personalities and talked to me.

But my life veered in a different course when I was 14 during one of the times I was off probation and living in Marysville — I committed a felony which put me on a fast track toward a criminal lifestyle.

One afternoon I skipped school with my girlfriend. We went to her house and hung out drinking beer with her mom. The mom wanted more beer and was too drunk to drive to get it herself. So she told me to take her Ford station wagon and get more. I was under-age, but there were winos around who would take a few dollars to purchase alcohol for us.

I had been drinking but wasn't over-the-top yet. As I passed in front of the high school, a guy driving a brand new Ranchero pulled out in front of me. I found out later he'd only had it one day. I hit his tailgate with such force that his car wrapped around a telephone pole. Guess whose it was? It was the principal of my high school. In the commotion with all the kids swarming around, I got out in a hurry and blended into the crowd – so I thought – then ran.

Later that night I made it home and acted like nothing happened. I lay down on my bed and went to sleep. The next morning I woke up to being handcuffed to the bed with my room full of cops. I was under arrest for felony hit and run, not to mention that I was an under-aged, unlicensed driver.

I was sentenced to one year in California Youth Authority – Camp Erwin Owen was a children's prison in Bakersfield, California. But all that did was give me a whole education about criminal activity.

I learned how to deal drugs without getting caught. I learned about the way police work. I networked with seasoned criminals and learned the tricks of the trade. I was 14 – but most of the kids in there were much older than me, up to 18-years-old. These boys had a lot more experience on the streets than I did and taught me everything they knew.

I also learned how to spot undercover agents and how police follow you. Back in those days it was real easy to spot if you were being tailed because police didn't have the smarts like today. And I learned how to tell if an undercover agent was trying to set somebody up.

For example, I stayed away from doing any kind of deal with people that I didn't know or with people who weren't highly recommended to me. I think that was part of my success in dealing drugs later and not getting caught. I had other people sell them for me, and I never sold to strangers.

Going to the Youth Authority gave me a clearer picture of where I was headed. I saw boys that were big, buff and had muscle. They worked out with weights – there were some big kids in there. I had two choices: become a part of them, or be scared so bad that I never, ever wanted to come back. I just learned how to be smarter.

Sure, the purpose of going to a place like that was to rehabilitate and learn how to be a good citizen; but it did the opposite. After doing a year in CYA, I came out knowing how to run an efficient, smart, criminal enterprise on the street.

I didn't need a "regular" job. I'd started selling drugs at age 13 in Marysville and San Francisco.

At age 15, I had a degree in my profession courtesy of the California Youth Authority system.

CHAPTER 3

A Hardening Heart

After I was released from Camp Erwin Owen, I went back to Marysville. I tried going to high school again, but I was more interested in the "high" part. My mom finally emancipated me when I was 16 and I happily skipped back to San Francisco. I didn't graduate and I didn't care.

It was easy to make money peddling drugs in San Francisco – it was the drug capital of the country at that time. I also sold an underground newspaper on the streets to chip in money for food and drugs. During my time dealing in Haight-Ashbury over the years, I made friends with hippies who lived in Monterey, so that's where I headed when I turned 18. About two years later I got married.

After a while I had a real good enterprise going on the Monterey Peninsula. Life was parties, drugs and rock concerts. I sold marijuana and cocaine and other types of drugs. I had a house on the beach, motorcycles and nice hippie vans. I was a gun freak so my house was full of guns. The kind of life that I lived meant that I always carried a gun. When you're doing a drug deal you could be robbed of the drugs you have to sell or of the cash you carry.

By this point, I'd been away from my mom and her abuse for several years. But I kept doing drugs because I still needed an escape from the reality of the pain that stayed with me because of her cruelty. I was about 25-years-old when I finally understood and accepted the fact that the reason that I kept doing it was because I was escaping the pain of my childhood. I was still hurt. It was also around this time that I found and contacted my father who coldly showed no interest. I honestly don't know if it would have made any difference if he had. By then, the lifestyle was ingrained in me.

I have been asked if it's possible that at some point I could have just gotten over the abusive years and lived a normal life; at what point was it my choice to keep getting high? At what point was I masking the suffering? People have suggested that I should have just gotten over it.

In my case — even though I came to grips with the abuse and with the way things were when I was a child — the drugs and that lifestyle had a firm hold on me. I had traded in my old family for a new family who seemed to really care about *me*. I thought they really had my back. Later I found out the bottom line: when the rubber met the road, they didn't have my back at all.

While I was living the good life on the Monterey Peninsula, my wife and I were having troubles and weren't getting along very good. The emotional upheaval really weighed on me.

One night I was at a party with 20 or 30 people. I walked into a bathroom and two guys were injecting heroin. I said, "Oh, excuse me!" and started to shut the bathroom door. One of my friends said, "Hey Cody, do you want a little?"

The worst mistake I ever made in my life. I said, "Yes." I put the needle in my arm.

I just wanted to see what it felt like.

It wasn't what I expected. The first time that you do heroin it makes you so sick. I only did four drops – about $3 or $4 worth. I started to sweat profusely, I threw up. That's the way it works. Before it even hits your stomach you're throwing up. I mean, you can't even take a drink of water. Your body is telling you that you've been poisoned. It made me so sick. But it put me in such euphoria. When it was over, I wanted that feeling again.

Every addict has told me this – heroin made them feel so sick, and yet they went back for more. It just doesn't make sense to anybody else. Other people don't understand that during those times of getting sick, you're waiting for that point to come when you couldn't care less about anything. From there, it doesn't matter what has happened in your life. You just can't think about it because you're in another place. As I became hooked I picked fights with my wife so that I could go storming out of the house and get heroin.

Little by little I became more and more and more addicted. I went from using one time, to using once every day, to using twice a day, then three times a day, four times a day, to 10 baggies a day. I had the means to buy a lot of drugs.

Of course, because I was doing that I didn't pay attention to my drug business. It went south. I just kept going lower and lower. Little by little, I sold everything that I had in order to get heroin into my system. I even peddled my gun collection. I lost my big house on the beach for a cheap little house in Seaside about two miles north of Monterey.

I was going down, down, down. I was arrested on six DUI charges throughout my career as a bad boy. The first time they jailed me for 30 days. After that it was a year in jail every time I got caught. I was so high on heroin once that I totaled my car. On that last arrest, the judge finally told me, "Cody, if you come before me with another DUI, you're going to be the first person ever sent to state prison for driving under the influence." So I quit doing that for a while.

From that point I started doing residential burglaries and stealing from "associates" because I ran out of my own things to sell. There are some real nice homes in real nice neighborhoods on the Monterey Peninsula: Carmel-by-the-Sea, Pacific Grove, Big Sur.

I was so desperate for heroin that I bought a Holiday Inn master key from an associate. I actually went around knocking on the doors of rooms. If nobody answered, I used the master key to go in and steal the color TV.

I had connections that would take merchandise in exchange for drugs. I could smuggle a computer, a real nice cell phone, a gun – whatever – to a dope dealer's house. They wouldn't give me anywhere near the value of it, but I walked out with drugs. I didn't care if it was a fair exchange. That wasn't my interest.

From my drug business, I got to know a lot of people who bought pounds of weed or cocaine from me. I knew what they had in their homes. And I knew that I could make a lot of money from taking their things – especially from gun collections, stereo equipment and stuff like that.

It wasn't long before I was a wanted man in the underworld community on the Monterey Peninsula.

The police eventually found me and got me for the 44 color TVs I'd stolen from Holiday Inn. When I was arrested, they also found a hypodermic needle and heroin in my back pocket. I did 30 days in the Salinas County Jail.

Because I was in jail for 30 days, I had no access to heroin. When I got out I made up my mind to stay off drugs; I'd been clean for a month. My life was out of control and I wanted to clean it up.

I thought about going back to Monterey, but that wasn't a smart option. In fact, it was dangerous. Half the town wanted to kill me. Seriously — not just beat me up — kill me. My connections included law enforcement employees who bought drugs from me and sold them to California prison officials. I knew a lot of heavy-duty people on the Peninsula in the 1970s.

For one thing, I knew that everyone carried guns. I'd already been shot at and stabbed and gang-jumped during fights. But I've never had a .44 Magnum bullet inside of me. The prospect wasn't exciting.

I decided to keep a wide berth from Monterey.

CHAPTER 4

Time in the Big House

While I was in the Salinas County jail, my wife moved in with another man and filed for divorce. In addition to being "most wanted" there really was no reason for me to stay in the area. Besides, truthfully, I was afraid.

So I hitchhiked to San Diego without a penny in my pocket.

When I arrived, I went to a beach and started robbing people. Simple as that. I got established with an apartment and a car, met people on the beach and got deeper into illegal activities. Then I heard about a steady job opening with the mob.

My mob contact operated with me to commit burglaries. If someone owed him money, he'd find out when they were going to be out of town for a while — say the Bahamas for a weekend. He had a guy who helped me get around alarm systems. With that information, I could go in and steal whatever I wanted.

I made my living like that for quite a while combined with dealing drugs on the beach. I was making pretty good money again; I only needed to break and enter once a month or so.

But I got caught. The beach house had a silent alarm that nobody knew about. Imagine my surprise when I crawled out of the kitchen window and saw that the whole block was surrounded by police — flashing lights, officers crouched on one knee with their guns aimed at me – the works. So I surrendered. It was either that or get shot. It was a no-brainer that I'd go to jail again.

Up until then, jail time for me had been for a lot of petty stuff like running away from home, driving under the influence and the 30 days in Salinas for burglary. I'd never been incarcerated for more than one year at a time. After this arrest I cooled my heels in a jail cell waiting to see a judge.

I found out that I was in big trouble this time — no jail for me. I was sentenced to one to 15 years in a state penitentiary – prison. All I heard the judge say was 15 years. I was 25. I didn't hear the *one* to 15. So I'm thinking, *Man, I'm gonna be like 40-years-old by the time I get out of there.*

The morning after sentencing I was handcuffed, shackled and dispatched to Chino, California on a prison bus. Getting off the bus at Chino and going through processing was a real eye-opener. I remember that day just like it was yesterday when those thick, heavy, metal doors opened to take me into the prison itself. I was caged with murderers, rapists and pedophiles. The place was full of animals. I mean it — just animals. Guys sat around and talked about the sickest stuff. I can't tell anyone what I heard because I don't even want those words to come across my lips. It was perverted stuff about how they had hurt people.

It was frightening. If it wasn't for my mob connection, I would've been in really bad trouble because I was good-looking with long, blonde hair. Thank God the mob had put the word out before I even got there, "Don't mess with Cody because he's one of our boys." It kept me from being raped and beaten. I only got into one fight; a guy came up and held a razor blade to my neck because he wanted my pack of cigarettes. I beat him up.

For some reason the judge chose me for an 11-68. That is where the sentencing judge kept jurisdiction over an inmate for one year with the possibility of early release. If you weren't called up, you became property of the state of California after that first year and chances were that you'd serve pretty close to your full sentence.

Every day a list was posted. Past my 300-day mark I got up every morning to see if I'd been recalled to San Diego.

During that year, the Aryan Brotherhood tried to recruit me into their gang. To get into the AB you had to stick a black guy and I didn't want to be affiliated with any of that gang activity going on in there. I told them I had a chance to be out in a year and I wasn't interested. The guy who tried to recruit me said we'd talk again when I became property of the state of California.

After 364 days my name was on the list.

So they sent me back to San Diego. They put me on three years' probation and released me. I've spent eight years of my life locked up but I'm happy to say that it was the only time I've been to prison.

Back at home in San Diego, I had a girlfriend who was a private duty nurse and had a place at the beach. She wasn't a user – she was in love with me and wanted to see me turn my life around. So I went out and got regular jobs to please my probation officer and her and tried to follow all the rules. I didn't want to give anybody any reason to send me back to prison.

I opened up a detail shop for cars. I cleaned and buffed vehicles at used car lots. But I hadn't really straightened up much. I started selling drugs again and burglarized because I needed money, man. I wasn't making enough money to keep me in the lifestyle I was used to. There isn't a whole lot of money detailing cars.

My girlfriend was making really good money in Rancho Santa Fe as a private nurse for rich people. She was really nervous that I was going to get arrested again, so she suggested that I go to nursing school.

The only jobs available for people coming out of nursing school at that time were night shifts. I really liked the idea of going into millionaire's homes, working from seven o'clock at night 'til seven in the morning — the only work involved was getting them ready for bed, putting them into bed, and getting them a drink of water when they woke up.

With that in mind, I started taking classes. But I found that I really liked nursing. After I graduated, I went for more training at Scripps Memorial Hospital in La Jolla and got my Licensed Practical Nurse certificate. Scripps is prestigious and one of the most famous hospitals in the greater San Diego area. That looked really good on my resume. People would automatically hire me because I'd had good training.

Here I was: someone who didn't graduate from high school but finished my nursing courses. Because I trained with Scripps and had that on my resume, no one did a background check to see that I was a convicted felon that they were going to let into millionaire's homes.

In those days, employers didn't do criminal checks. I worked for famous people whose names you'd recognize. When I added their names and the private duty work I did for them onto my resume, I got nearly every job that I applied for. They always gave me good references. Most of my work was in Rancho Santa Fe, an exclusive community near Del Mar in northern San Diego County. I ended up working there for about 10 years.

Because I was busy with work that I enjoyed, I'd get to a place where I thought I had gotten rid of my drug problem; I really thought it was all gone. I made really good money and bought whatever I wanted to buy and did whatever I wanted to do. But the problem was that every time something emotional happened in my life I'd go back to drugs. I'd get close to a patient and they would die. After four years, my girlfriend and I broke up. So I never really left drugs behind – they were the only friends I really had, so I always turned to them. I didn't know how to deal with loss at all. Every time there was an upheaval in my life I went back to drugs. Always.

A lot of drug addicts have this mindset: drugs never let them down. People always let them down, but not drugs.

Drugs are faithful to hide or mask feelings. They hide that heartache for a little while.

Looking back, I can see that I had so many emotional issues that subconsciously I hoped that the next injection would kill me — that the next hit would end the pain forever. I wouldn't have any more pain and I wouldn't have to worry about being arrested and put back in prison or anything else. At that point, I had no clue about Heaven and Hell. I was a big, bad guy. I thought, *Well, hey, if your loving God's just gonna send me to Hell, so be it. I'll be kicked into the fire and burned up.* I didn't realize that Hell lasts forever and there is no way out.

After the breakup I went back to using cocaine or whatever else I could find. I rode with outlaw motorcycle clubs, too. I lived two different lives. I worked all week then partied on the weekends. My life was all about motorcycles, drugs and girls. These days it's called being a functional addict. I was out of control on weekends but no one knew.

I never used drugs on the job. I worked with millionaires, took them to doctor appointments and meetings, and I needed to be clear-headed. For the first time in my life I wore suits and slacks and dress-up hoity-toity clothes because it was part of my job. On weekends I got down and dirty.

Functional addicts don't go through physical withdrawals of doing drugs. For example, I got off work on Friday night, did drugs from then through the weekend and stopped on Sunday afternoon. When I went back to work on Monday, I wasn't looking too good. I'd just tell people I had a rough weekend. They'd say, "God, Cody, you look tired." I wasn't off the drugs long enough to have physical withdrawal with stomach cramps and sweating and all the other stuff that comes with it.

One of my favorite patients was Maynard E. Montrose, Howard Hughes' right hand man; people called him Monty. Monty was very rich and powerful. I took care of him at his home in Rancho Santa Fe for about five years; I really enjoyed his company. When he died, my default setting kicked in and I didn't handle it well. His passing was a catalyst to getting back on heroin.

Around that time I ran into a guy in San Diego who had a contact to get heroin and I began to use again. Heroin has an addictive power, but it's not just physically. It's a comfort place in your mind. I was off of my probation, so I didn't have to worry about getting tested by my Probation Officer.

Normal people wonder why I would pick up heroin again. They'd say, "Man, this guy really went through hell. Why would he ever do that again?" It's because I was having an emotional problem and I went back to the only true friend that I knew — and that was heroin. That doesn't make sense to anybody but a drug addict. It really doesn't.

When I started using again, I did the same pattern. I used it one time. Then once a week. Then twice a week, then twice a day, and it really got out of control. This time I got really addicted – worse than before. I went through all of my savings and started to lose everything I'd worked so hard for.

Finally, I got to the point that I went to a methadone clinic. I was still working and needed to grab control of myself. I was back in the mindset of wondering where I was going to get my dope for the next day, and I was tired of chasing that. Methadone helped me to get off heroin; but then I got addicted to methadone.

By now I'd been in San Diego for several years. I knew everybody at the beach. In a community like that, no one drives – they're all outdoors on skates or skateboards or bicycles or just walking. So we all get to know each other. I knew who I could sell to, who I couldn't sell to.

And I wasn't really having money problems anymore. I was not working a regular job but I was involved in the underworld again doing burglaries, selling drugs, getting the heroin that I needed. Life was nothing but a dangerous party.

My problem was that I wanted to start over.

I wanted to get away from getting high. It was almost impossible because I couldn't walk down the street without somebody saying, "Hey Cody! Come on, let's get high!" No matter how much I tried to quit, I couldn't because of all the people I knew and the people that I had taken care of over the years. It just got insane – I couldn't get away from it.

So I came up with a brilliant idea. I decided to move to another city where I didn't know anybody and I couldn't buy heroin.

My bright idea was to move to Las Vegas.

CHAPTER 5

Getting Too Hot in Vegas

I was just shy of 46-years-old when I arrived in Las Vegas in May 1997. It was already hot.

I was sick as a dog from withdrawal. I was vomiting, shaking, sweating – just sick. I had severe diarrhea and couldn't get drugs out of my mind; I knew that if I got heroin into my body, I would be well. I needed some drugs.

I went to Binion's Horseshoe casino in the morning to get some beer because it relieves withdrawal symptoms a little. So I slowly made it up to the bar and ordered a beer. There was already a guy sitting there and he started a conversation. He asked what I was doing in Vegas and I answered with small talk.

Finally he asked why I was there at the casino, and in the end I just told him, "Well, I'm an addict, man, I'm trying to get away from drugs."

He looked at me and said, "Well, do you want to get well?" In drug-speak that means, "Do you want to get high?" And I'm like, "Yeah. I want to get high."

My new dealer lived two blocks away in an apartment with his girlfriend.

And here we go again.

But this time I got involved in a counterfeiting ring.

When I came to Vegas I had some money in savings, but I was quickly running out of it. The guy who initially gave me drugs kept selling them to me whenever I needed them, but I was getting low on money. One day we were talking, and I told him, "Man, I don't know what I'm gonna do." It was getting to the point that I didn't know if I'd be able to keep a roof over my head.

My supplier also turned out to be part of a gang who ran a counterfeit ring in Vegas. I didn't know it, but they had done a background check on me to find out if I was an undercover cop or someone trying to infiltrate their ring. I could have been FBI, Nevada State Gaming Control or Las Vegas Metropolitan Police.

One day he said, "Hey, Cody, I know some guys who have a really good way of making money here in Las Vegas." My first question was, "Is it legal?" He said, "No, but it's pretty much foolproof."

He was part of a five-member gang and they were short a crew member. So I met with them in a motel room. They told me what they did and how much money I would make and asked if I would agree to enter their training program. I was like, "Training program? What is this?"

They used lead to create fake silver dollars to drop into slot machines in casinos all over the city. They told me that they would show me all the ins and outs of how to operate. But they warned me several times that I would face certain death if I violated any of their rules. And I totally believed them. The leader of this racket was an ex-Navy seal. His job was to take out security if any of us ever got jacked up in a casino. They were very serious about their little enterprise.

So I went into training for six months.

Sleight-of-hand was a big part of what we did, so I practiced a lot. For example, if a machine took five coins, which in those days a lot of them did, I practiced at home how to manipulate the coins as fast as I could into the slot. I trained my thumb, index finger and middle finger to move really quick and drop them into the machine. It's something all of us practiced all the time because time is of the essence; we wanted to get in and get out with their money before they even knew we were there.

In order for that aspect of what we did to work, we each had a "blocker." When I worked the machines, my blocker stood in front of the security camera so they couldn't identify us. So I'd play for a little bit, just long enough to look like I was gambling then cash out. I'd drop a couple hundred fake dollars into the machine and take the real dollars that dropped out and put them in my little cup and cash them in. We didn't go in there, put 200 coins in, then hit "cash out" because that would look suspicious. We had to play for a little bit.

But we also had to be careful not to hit it big. When someone hits the big jackpot like the big sevens or a royal flush on a poker machine, the first thing casino employees do is open up the machines to recalibrate and check all the coins that are in there. Our coins were totally perfect on one side — side by side they looked the same with the eagle on one side and you couldn't tell the difference. But the other side was blank. So if a machine was opened up and they saw a bunch of blank coins sitting there, I would have been jacked up.

So if I played poker and got dealt four cards to the royal, I kept a jack and threw everything else away and redrew because I never wanted to hit a big jackpot and have them come running up to open the machine.

In 1997-1998, it cost us about seven cents to make one counterfeit silver dollar. We'd go out and drop them in the machines of all the major casinos and bars in Las Vegas. We kept odds on and kept extensive books on how much we made. In those days we were getting well over 90 percent of what we played.

But even with blockers, the longer I was in the casino cheating, the more time they had to identify me and put somebody watching me. So I was deceptive — always changing my looks and the way I dressed so that I wouldn't be identifiable. One day I'd wear a shirt and a sport coat with a pair of jeans and cowboy boots, and then another time I wore a Hawaiian shirt and shorts. I always switched up my style of dress, facial hair, haircuts — growing a moustache, shaving it off, growing a beard, shaving it off, trying to look different every time so I couldn't be identified.

But you know, they eventually did identify us. Gangs like ours are one reason that casinos use paper now.

Even with the success of our "business," we didn't have growing bank accounts. We all used heroin. We made anywhere from 2,000 to 2,500 coins in the space of about six hours with all five of us working. We made $1,500 to $1,700 a night, then go buy dope with it. We got high all night, saved some heroin to use in the morning when we woke up, and did the whole thing all over again. We made a lot of money, but all of us used and that wasn't a good thing. That just wasn't a good thing.

After working with these guys for about six months I figured that I could do this on my own. I'd rather split it one way than five ways. So I disappeared.

By this time, the FBI, Metropolitan Police, Nevada Gaming Control, and United States Marshals were all after me, but they couldn't find me. They knew who I was, but I was real slick. When I operated I wore disguises and changed locations frequently. I was real good at moving around and staying hidden.

After a while I was too hot in Vegas. My picture — mug shots and surveillance photos — were in every casino and every gaming bar in the whole town. I almost got caught a couple times, so I went out to Bullhead City and stayed there. I made my coins during the week and went to Las Vegas on the weekend. I usually went back home with anywhere from $5,000 to $8,000.

After a while I felt the heat and was terrified of going back to prison. I was on the FBI Most Wanted list; my picture was everywhere. So I called an attorney. I told him the whole story and asked, "What would happen if I turn myself in?

Will I go to prison?" He promised me, "Cody, I can guarantee you that if you hire me as your attorney you will only do one year county jail time, not prison."

So I agreed and asked for three weeks to take care of my business. By then I had boats and a motor home and cars all under alias names. After three weeks I went to Vegas and turned myself in. What my attorney promised is exactly what happened — I got one year in jail. They dropped the possession of illegal coin because I didn't have any on me when I surrendered.

District Court Judge Stephen Huffaker told me that if I ever came before him again on a gaming charge he would put me so far into prison, "They'll have to shoot beans to you from a cannon." I took him very seriously.

I was so used to being in jail by then it was no big deal; there wasn't anyone to visit me or anything. After prison, jail was like going to a playpen. One year of jail wasn't anything.

After I served my time I got three years' probation – but I got off that early because I was doing real good. I got into private duty nursing again and also registered with a nursing agency, so I worked for every hospital in Vegas: Sunrise, UMC, Mountain View — all of them. When somebody didn't show up at a hospital for a shift, someone from staff would call the nursing agency and the agency called me and sent me out to the hospital.

During this time I took up pro bass fishing and made good money. Fishing had been a passion of mine that started with my step-dad in northern California. Throughout the years I kept it as a hobby and enjoyed both fresh and saltwater angling. When I lived in San Diego I'd go on long-range trips down to Mexico.

I started fishing the bass club events and winning a lot. Then I graduated to Western Outdoor News (WON) bass events and competed in tournaments from Vegas to Lake Meade and Lake Havasu, Arizona. For years, I participated in the US Open on Lake Mead. In fact, I was pretty famous.

While I was fishing and working I still did drugs, but they were under control. I broke my leg from a misstep I took when I was high, and was on hiatus from nursing when Mimi, an 80-year-old Christian, needed an in-house private duty nurse and contacted the agency I worked for. No one was available but me, and they told her I was qualified but wouldn't be up and about for a while.

Mimi said she didn't care and hired me. During my first month in her home, she took care of me because I was unable to do anything but lay on the couch with my leg up. I was also on methadone again and Mimi paid for it until I was off of it.

After I healed, I took care of her. I thought that she should know about my past, so she heard my whole story. I was in my late 40s by then. She said, "Well Cody, you know what? All of that is in your past, and I thank you for telling me, but it doesn't make any difference to your employment here. God forgives you and I forgive you."

Over the five years that I lived with her and took care of her, Mimi became the grandma that I never had. She forgave my bad past, gave me moral guidance and was a great role model. I cooked her meals, cleaned her house, mowed her yard. She went with me on pre-fishing trips to Lake Mead before upcoming tournaments, too. The other competitors loved her; she oozed comfort and peace toward everyone. To tell the truth, this period of my life was the longest I had ever stayed away from drugs.

Mimi became my only family. I thought I'd had a family with people in motorcycle clubs and other friends that I hung out with, but Mimi treated me like her grandson. I never had a grandma, but I thought of her as my grandma. I really did. She was the nicest, sweetest little lady that you'd ever meet.

But then Mimi developed dementia.

What does that signal? An emotional upheaval, right? I was devastated.

One night I walked into a friend's house; he was smoking a crack pipe. I said, "Could I have a hit of that?" He tried his very best to talk me out of it. I had a brand new bass boat, a brand new truck, and a good job that paid me $1,000 a week. I was going all over the place for fishing tournaments and I thought my drug problem was all over. I still remember his name – Ron. He tried his very best to talk me out of it. But I insisted, "No, give me a hit."

So he did. And here we go again — because I was watching Mimi slowly lose her mind.

Once Mimi's dementia progressed I started using crack regularly. Oh my God, I thought heroin was addictive. Crack is much more so. You get to the point that you want to smoke it at least every hour. Every time you smoke it, you just want more, and more, and more.

Mimi ended up going completely berserk and died about six months later. That's when I went off the deep end. Because I smoked crack regularly, I started losing everything. Again.

I had a lot of money saved up from winning fishing tournaments and from putting money aside. I didn't just sell drugs all the time. I mean, I did for a lot of the time but not all of the time. That's not where *all* my money came from. But I wanted more crack and sold my brand new, $45,000 Ranger bass boat that I had just bought. I drove that boat to Lake Havasu and sold it to a guy for $13,000 so I could buy drugs.

It was an endless cycle. Emotional turmoil was my trigger and I was self-destructive. A prison test verified that fact.

When you're admitted to prison, you're given a test. It's called the Minnesota Multiphasic Aptitude Test. Each inmate has to answer 500 questions and it takes about two days to do it. Psychologists can figure out your personality disorder from the way that you answer the questions – why you're a criminal. The test can tell why you're a convict, why you're a drug addict, why you're a pervert, why you are whatever you are. I was really surprised at my result: Cody is self-destructive.

I thought about that; I was self-destructive. Something good could happen to me, but when that really good thing ended I went back to drugs. I went back to the only friend that I knew — heroin.

Now crack cocaine joined my circle of friends.

CHAPTER 6

The Whole World is Evil, Except for the McDonald's Lady

Before I knew it, I spent – and I'm not kidding – I spent $1,000 a day on crack. I had yard sales to sell all of my stuff so that I could buy drugs. It didn't take me long to burn through my life savings.

Normal people think, *Well, this guy had to see this coming*. And I did because I started getting notices from banks that I was overdrawn on credit cards, that I was cashing bad checks and sometimes I was arrested and did jail time for that. I knew everything was coming to an end. But when you're on drugs, you don't realize how close it is until the end comes.

In summer 2002 a marshal came with an eviction notice to the place where I lived. I had five days to get out. I looked around and thought, *Okay, I'm not going to have a place to live so what am I going to do?* So I got a backpack and shoved in some jeans and t-shirts, a jacket, and a toothbrush and toothpaste and other things I thought I might need because I didn't have anywhere to go — but I forgot a sleeping bag. I left because if I didn't leave, I was going to get arrested. With a record like mine, I *had* to leave.

I remember that day very well. It was really hot: 110 degrees in Las Vegas.

When I walked out of the house and into the blazing heat, I went about four blocks over on Boulder Highway to Budget Suites. Some homeless men were there. I introduced myself, "My name's Cody. I became homeless today; could I ask you a few questions?" I asked, "How do you eat?" "Where do you go to the bathroom?" "Where do you get cleaned up?" "Where do you sleep without the police bothering you?" You know, basic survival skill-type questions. I got all kinds of answers, so I went on a gut feeling of what would work out best for me.

I ended up down on Fremont Street and Eastern not far from the Odyssey Bar. There was a dirt field behind the police station and I made a place in the flowering oleander bushes where I could crawl in and sleep at night.

My new place was also convenient. There were about 30 little motels all around there with crack dealers. I camped out real close to where my drugs were.

I got so strung out that I didn't want to live anymore. I was in basic survival mode but I hoped that the next hit of crack would stop my heart. I didn't want to be homeless, I didn't want to be where I was; I didn't want to be an addict. But there was no way out.

Day by day I lost more self-esteem, especially when I'd walk into a fast food place to use the bathroom or to cool off for a few minutes. Wherever I went, people stopped me at the door and said, "You're not welcome here."

One time when I wanted to use a public telephone, the police pulled up with red lights flashing and told me that I couldn't be on the property. I said, "I'm using the phone." The officer told me that I couldn't use that phone and pointed to a sign that read "For Public Use Only." I asked, "Aren't I the public?" He said, "No, you're not the public anymore."

Stuff like that begins to gnaw at you until your self-esteem is obliterated.

I was so involved in drugs that I only slept once every three days anyway. I kinda got to the point where I just accepted that I'm homeless and I'm just gonna die out here. Somebody's gonna kill me or cut my throat. I just didn't have any hope. I didn't have any hope at all. When the weather turned cold I dug smelly, tattered blankets out of trash cans. When it rained, I found painter's plastic sheets to drape over myself and my things, but nothing really kept the cold and wet out. And when it was hot, there was no way to cool off. I adjusted to life on the streets, but I hated it.

I saw some of the most horrible things. I saw gangs shoot people, I saw people robbed, I saw people beaten within an inch of their lives. I saw violence like I had never seen before – and I had a pretty tough life growing up. I saw brutality over the stupidest, dumbest things like drunks getting into fights and stabbing one another over a woman, or food, or booze.

One thing that I could never wrap my head around was that homeless people stole from each other. I mean, why?

We were all in the same boat, we all had nothing. And yet they robbed each other. That's what blew me away more than anything.

The attitude of a lot of the police was awful. I couldn't sit at a bus stop, I couldn't walk across the street, I couldn't use a public phone without being harassed. And they harassed me every couple of days for no good reason. I was arrested a lot for stupid stuff like being a vagrant, trespassing on private property, loitering in a public place — which was sitting at a bus stop. I know there are a lot of good police officers too, but there are some that treat homeless people worse than a dog. It really opened my eyes.

Sometimes people gunned their cars like they were going to run me down when I crossed the street. I developed a mindset that the whole world was evil. I really did. I saw it from the police, I saw it from business owners, I saw it from all types of people.

Every once in a while someone hired me to paint a fence or pull weeds. One guy on Boulder Highway took a liking to me and let me sweep up his glass shop. Every week he'd give me one day's work. I'd get paid and buy drugs with it. I ran into a few nice people, but mostly I was convinced that nobody cared — and I didn't care. I didn't care if I lived or died.

Before this, although I'd been in and out of jail and gained and lost mountains of money, I had always managed to take care of myself without begging. And I determined that I would not beg.

After my first night of being homeless, I was really hungry. I asked a man if he could give me a couple dollars so I could get a hamburger. He told me to get a job. Well I just totally went off on him and he called the police, 'cause I guess he was afraid of me.

I never begged again. I couldn't be a beggar.

I adjusted to being homeless and found a way to supply my crack habit. I ran into another homeless man who was also a drug addict, and he had this thing with washing the windows on cars. So I took the idea from him, got a bottle of Windex, and found out that you can make pretty good money doing that.

I would "go to work" three days at a time and wash windows 24/7 for a donation. I got a bus pass and went to a shopping center to wash windows until somebody complained and the manager kicked me out. Then I'd get on another bus and go to the next shopping center. Sometimes I walked if I could or worked my way along whatever boulevard I was on until I had enough money to get back down to Fremont Street and buy more dope.

All my money went toward dope. I wouldn't feed myself. I wouldn't even stop and spend $1 to buy a hamburger at McDonald's. I mean, I was a smoker and picked cigarette butts up off the street and smoked them rather than spend $1 on a cheap pack of cigarettes.

On a good day, I made anywhere between $100 and $150. As soon as I got $50 or $60 in my pocket I got on the bus and went to where I knew I could get drugs — any of those 30 little hotels on Fremont Street, not far from my oleander bush home. It took me about 10 minutes to smoke through $50 of dope.

When no one stopped me from getting on a bus, I wasn't interested in what people thought. I wasn't concerned about,

"Am I clean?" or "Do I smell?" or "Are my teeth brushed?" All I thought about was survival and getting enough money for my next hit. There are times that I'm sure people thought I was totally crazy. Occasionally people would get up and move away because I smelled so bad. Sometimes I had enough and stood up to yell at people. I said, "It's real easy for you to make fun of me because you have a place to take a shower and I don't. I'm homeless." I acted totally insane.

Even Mexicans — and Mexican people were usually very nice to me when I was homeless – got the brunt of my anger. I know a little bit of Spanish so when they said, "He smells," I understood what they said. When I heard it, I turned around and yelled at them, too.

It wasn't just people on the bus that I yelled at. I got angry at people and yelled for many reasons: I felt like they were making fun of me, that they didn't care about me, that they despised me. I believed that no one cared. I was angry because of the situation that I was in. And then there was the fact that I didn't care anymore; I didn't care if I got beat up, I didn't care if somebody killed me.

One day I walked up to a man sitting in his car at Denny's on Boulder Highway. He was older, probably about 65. I was going to ask if I could clean his windows. Well, he rolled down his window, stuck a .9 millimeter in my face and said, "Back away from my car or I'll shoot!" Instead of backing away, I got closer and it scared the living crap out of him. I yelled and screamed at him, "You know what? Go ahead! Pull the trigger! Put me out of my misery! *Pull the trigger!*"

He threw his car in reverse and took off instead of shooting me. But at that moment, I didn't have anything else to live for; I really wished that he *had* pulled the trigger.

The interesting thing is that because I worked for my drug money, I had a little bit of dignity left. In my mind, nobody could say I didn't have a job. If anyone said to me, "Why don't you go get a job?" my reply was, "I have a job. That's why I'm asking you, 'Can I clean the windows on your car?' I'm providing a service for you." That's how whacked I was; I didn't believe that I was begging if I offered to do a service.

Sometimes washing people's windows was really cool. People in Las Vegas are not known for being nice to homeless people, but every once in a while someone would ask me, "What's your name?" It brought tears to my eyes to hear that question because it meant that someone still thought of me as a real person. That was a rare question right there; nobody in Vegas wants to know your name. I'd say "Cody." Sometimes they were interested and said, "Cody, could I ask you a few questions? Man, how did this happen to you?" And I told them the truth. I wasn't one to come up with a big story like a lot of homeless people who said that they were a victim of circumstances. I told them, "I'm a drug addict."

I was also surprised when people asked my name while I cleaned the windows on their car, because part of my hustle was that the more I smelled, the more people felt sorry for me and handed me money to send me on my way. I believed that nobody wanted to become involved with me; they wanted to keep me at arm's length. I didn't blame those who did. I was dirty, smelly, and horrible-looking and I knew it.

Sometimes, not a whole lot of time, I ran across people who had a heart. They said, "Well, hey man, if you're hungry, I'll take you over to Subway," or "I'll buy you a sandwich, I'll get you a Coke," "If you're hungry, why don't you wait right here? I'll get you something to eat and I'll bring it back to you." It was those moments that gave me a glimmer of hope that there were still good people. I never turned down food. I never said, "I just want money."

I can only imagine what people thought when they saw me. In Las Vegas, people work and get off at all different hours – they'd come out of a grocery store at three o'clock in the morning and here's some guy with a bottle of Windex wanting to clean their windows. They had to think, *This guy's nuts!*

But the way I looked at it was that at least I offered a practical service.

There were times when I tried to find a regular job. I got as normal-looking as I could. I used the bathroom at the park to clean myself up, shave, put on a clean t-shirt, and even used the dog water-nozzle to wash my hair. I still looked terrible, but I went out and tried. I offered to sweep, to paint, to do anything that needed to be done. Most business people just laughed at me and told me to leave before they called the police.

So I kept at my steady job of offering a service for window washing all over the glittering city.

In fact, that's how I met a lady named Heather.

I met Heather at an Albertson's shopping center. She had just pulled into a parking space in her little red car. I limped up to her, pretending to have a bad leg. Limping was another part of my strategy so people would think that I was a war veteran or broke my leg really bad.

Anyway, Heather's car had just been detailed, so she said, "No, Honey, I don't want you to clean my windows, but here..." and she handed me a $5 McDonald's gift certificate. There was a McDonald's right across the street. That really touched my heart that a woman would do such a nice thing. I was really hungry, too. After I ate a couple of hamburgers, fries and a Coke from the Dollar Menu, I had 12 cents left.

I found out later when we crossed paths again that handing out McDonald's food certificates was a regular thing for her. She would buy 100 of them at a time. All the homeless people called her the McDonald's Lady.

I know that making $100 to $150 per day washing windshields was good money – more than a lot of people with "real jobs" make. I have been asked, "How could you be homeless if you were making that much money?" Because I was a drug addict. I could never save money. I promised myself that if I could save X amount of dollars — if I could save $50 every day — I could get a weekly rental at a cheap motel. Or I could get this, or I could get that.

But the bottom line was the drug. I was addicted to crack cocaine and it had such a hold on me that I wouldn't even spend $1 on a hamburger much less $50 a day for a roof over my head. That $50 bought me 10 minutes of crack. Every penny that I made went to drugs.

It wasn't until that hot July night in the park when I practically crawled into the stinking, fly-blown dumpster across the street so that I could fill my empty belly with garbage scraps that I realized how far I'd fallen.

Many times over the previous 30 years I sat atop mountains of cash and squandered it all away. Many times. At 51 years old, I literally had nothing of value, not even myself. Where do you go, what do you do when all that you know is despair? I had spent nearly every hour of every day getting high — or working so that I could get high. At one point I even went to a mental hospital and told them I was crazy and needed help. They told me to leave — that I was just an addict.

Another time I went to a police officer on the street and begged him to take me to jail. After a few minutes of pleading, he ran my information on his computer and found out that there was a warrant for my arrest for trespassing so he took me to jail. I was so tired of being homeless. For a night or two I got a roof over my head even though the door was locked from the outside.

In society's eyes, I wasn't human. I was a stray dog – a nuisance. I was a problem that society had to deal with. Nobody looked at me like I was a person anymore. So I believed that I wasn't.

On my knees in a hot, stinking alley with my belly full of garbage, I *felt* like nothing more than an animal.

Part 2

CHAPTER 7

From a Dumpster
to a Feast

After my tears were spent, I mopped myself up and staggered back to my oleander bush bed in the dirt field. I lay there, looking at the sky easing into a pre-sunrise gray. I was so broken and so beat up from being on the street. I wasn't "me" anymore. I was mad. I was hateful. The last shreds of my dignity and self-respect were finally gone. Eventually I went back to sleep.

Normally in those days, dealers started riding their bicycles up and down Fremont Street about eight o'clock every morning. I slept until about seven o'clock, then went to hustle money so I could get high.

As I mentioned earlier, part of my hustle with window cleaning was to get as smelly as I could. The dirtier I looked, the more I smelled, the worse my beard was or however messy I appeared, people had compassion and let me do their car windows or just handed me money.

The funny thing is, I had a revelation: I didn't know that a human body could smell so bad. I mean, I just reeked. You could be 20 feet away and smell me — that's how bad I smelled. Even homeless people didn't want to be around me. They complained, "Hey Cody, you need to get cleaned up because you stink."

I got to the point where I was so skinny that you could count my ribs when I took off my shirt. I tied shoelaces around the waistband of my pants to hold them up. I was that skinny from not eating. I tried to keep myself hydrated but I didn't eat. I've seen pictures of people from the Holocaust, and that's what I looked like. I was a mess.

About three or four months later my friend Jim invited me to go with him to a church where we could take a shower, get cleaned up, get a pair of new socks and get some food. He invited me because I stunk – not because he was being nice.

In the park, Jim and his girlfriend Lori slept next to me. Their hustle was that she'd get pregnant then sell their babies underground for $10,000 apiece. It was a constant. She'd get pregnant, have the child and get off the streets for two or three months. They were both real bad alcoholics. They always ended up back on a park bench. They lived high on the hog drinking and gambling for a few months off the streets, then come back to the park.

My stench was especially noticeable to Jim and his girlfriend because I slept right next to them. I'd come back at night from pounding the streets all day looking for windshields to wash and take off my shoes — and I just smelled horrible. One day he said, "Oh my God Cody, do you want to go with me tomorrow to this church so you can take a shower and get cleaned up? Because man, you smell."

Well, clean, new socks were a huge deal to me because during the summertime in Vegas I walked a lot and my feet got really sweaty. If I wore the same pair of socks for three or four days, they literally stood up after they dried out after I took them off at night. I mean, I didn't even want to put them back on, they were so bad.

So I took Jim up on his offer and we went to Central Christian church the next day. It was on a Saturday in the middle of May when he asked me to go, so the day that we went was Sunday. We got up at 4 am to walk the seven miles to church. They opened the doors at 6 am and marched whoever was there to a waiting room upstairs where we took a number to get our shower and other supplies. They took six or seven guys at a time to shower. There was coffee and doughnuts for us to eat while we waited, and people to minister to or pray for us.

All I wanted was to get to the church, take a shower, get cleaned up, get clean clothes, eat, and get whatever else I could. I didn't want anything to do with God. I was certain that God had put me where I was – on the streets – as punishment for all the bad stuff that I had done in my life. I thought that God made me homeless. I was still angry at Him and I didn't want anything to do with the church or the Bible or any of that stuff.

While I waited I ate as many donuts as I could and drank coffee. Jim was the only one there that I knew, so I just sat there with him, stuffing my mouth with donuts and waiting for my number to be called. A lady named Michelle walked over and stood in front of me. I looked up at her. She said, "Excuse me, my name's Michelle." I said, "My name's Cody." Michelle said, "Honey, you look like you need a hug."

I was so filthy and so smelly and here's this little lady telling me that I need a hug. I shook my head and told her, "No, you don't wanna hug me because I smell too bad."

Michelle looked me in my eyes and said that I didn't smell. She said, "Come here and let me give you a hug." I stood up, and when she gave me that hug, she whispered three words in my ear: "Jesus loves you."

That totally blew my mind. So many thoughts started tumbling through my brain: *How could Jesus love me? I'm a drug addict. I've been a criminal all of my life. I have hurt people. I've stole from people.*

I stepped back, looked at her and said, "Jesus can't love me." I told her everything that I had just thought.

Michelle said, "Cody, do you know what? Forgiveness, mercy, and grace are available for you."

And I was like, "Really?" I didn't know anything about this. The love that I saw radiating from this woman's face made me want to know more about this Jesus that she talked about.

That day, we all took our showers and got cleaned up. They provided deodorant and hairdryers and everything. In fact, one of the volunteers who had seen me walk in saw me again after I was shaved and cleaned up. He said, "Man, Cody, you look so good, you look like you're going to play 18 holes of golf." Even though I brushed off his compliment with an abrupt, "Man, I don't golf, I'm not even interested in that stuff," his comment made me feel good. It stirred up thoughts like, *Wow, Cody, you look good, you know. You don't even look like the same guy that came through the door.* But I shut those thoughts down in a hurry.

After showers, volunteers fed us a breakfast of scrambled eggs and bacon. When we were fed, scrubbed up and presentable, we attended a Bible study for 20 or 30 minutes. As I sat down I really tried to close my ears to this talk about Jesus because I still felt that God was punishing me for the life that I'd led. I was angry with Him.

But the more I heard, the more Jesus touched my heart. And even though I tried not to hear it, I heard. I wanted to put my fingers in my ears like, *Nah, nah, nah, nah I don't believe this stuff.*

But my heart was touched.

Before the Bible study ended, something happened — like a switch went on, man. I wanted to know more about this Jesus who could forgive me of my sins, who could make me a new man. I wanted to know more.

They gave me a Bible. It's a beautiful, leather Bible. I'm guessing that it belonged to a little girl because there are all these little notes in it and drawings of little flowers and hearts. I still have the Bible here at my house.

But anyway, I left that day and all I could think about was, *Really? If all of that is available to me and it doesn't cost me a penny — all it costs is me being determined to know Jesus Christ and to turn my life over to Him —* I couldn't get it out of my mind. *I want that. I want that. If forgiveness and redemption and grace and mercy and love are available to me, I want that.*

I still hustled and got my drugs every day, but for the next three weeks I tried to cut back. I went back to church every Sunday and the homeless outreach and the Bible studies. I liked the chance to shower and have breakfast. And I found that I liked the Bible study – even though it wasn't required. I kept feeling this tugging at my heart every time I went back. It got stronger and stronger and stronger. I heard all these wonderful stories about Jesus and how He loves us and all the things that are available to a believer. But I kept being tempted by drugs and giving in.

Every Sunday I went back to church. After church, I went back to the dirt field. After three weeks I decided on my own to read the Bible that they gave me. I finally asked someone at church, "Where do I start reading?"

They told me to stay out of the Old Testament for now, and to begin with the story of Jesus starting in the book of Matthew, then Mark and Luke and John. After that, I was to read the Book of Acts to get a better understanding. And they told me to pray before I read because otherwise I wouldn't be able to understand anything.

Well, the more I read the Bible, the more I *wanted to* read the Bible. I still hadn't given my heart to Christ. The idea became more compelling when I saw that Jesus died on a cross for my sin…but this was all beyond my understanding. I read that Jesus took away the sin of the whole world, but that we had to accept it. Most of all, I struggled to grasp this one thing that someone told me, "Cody, you know what? If you were the only person on this earth, Christ would have died for you."

And man, I thought about stuff like that.

I read in the Bible about this horrible death that Jesus had to endure so that we could be forgiven and bought back, and so we could have life never-ending, so that we could have it lavishly. Then I read about temptation and deception and the enemy of our souls and all of that stuff. The more I read, the more things clicked and I started to understand what had happened to me throughout my whole life.

And I couldn't get enough. I couldn't get enough of reading the Bible. Before long, I started holding Bible studies at the field – and I didn't really know the first thing about Jesus. I read these stories and I'd be like, "Hey, you guys, come here, man, you gotta hear this!" And all the guys at the homeless park made fun of me. They said, "Hey, Cody really got some good crack, man. He's over there under the tree reading the Bible and he wants us all to listen."

But I didn't care. They could make fun of me all they wanted. The Book was starting to make sense. The more I read it, the more I understood. That went on for a couple of weeks. Then I began to feel the call. The Holy Spirit touched my heart — although at the time I didn't know it was Him — and I started to understand that I really needed Jesus to save me. I needed Him as my personal Lord and Savior.

Something was happening to my hardened, leathery heart.

I'm not proud of this, but there were times in my life that if somebody had offered me $10,000 to kill someone I would have done it. I used to think about it a lot. I didn't care who I hurt as long as I got what I wanted. That's how hard my heart was.

The Bible tells us that God will replace a heart of stone with a heart of flesh. Well, I began to feel my heart softening; tears ran down my face when I read stories about Jesus being crucified and the horrible pain and suffering that He went through so that everyone in the world—so that *I*— could be saved through Him from the grip of sin and misery. Adding to that, I found that people at the church really seemed to care about me.

So I came up with an idea: instead of being in a place all the time where I was tempted by drugs and all the stuff that goes along with it, starting on Monday I would go to church and ask people there if they had anything I could do to help. I would rather be at the church every day where people genuinely cared about me.

Another part of that is that I had cut back on doing drugs. Being at church kept me out of places where I was tempted. I knew that the enemy saw that I was taking steps toward the Lord, so he kept putting things in my path to pull me back into his realm. As new to the faith as I was, I knew that there was spiritual warfare going on. Thank God I followed up on my brainstorm and went to the church every day.

Picture this: there are a lot of offices at Central Christian, and I'd walk up to office doors, knock, peek in and say, "Hi, my name is Cody. I'm a homeless guy, but I'm going to turn my life over to the will of God. Is there anything I could do to help you?" Sometimes somebody was working on computers, and they'd ask me if I knew how to use one. I said, "No, but there's gotta be something I can do around here." You can imagine that they were pretty shocked.

One day I was upstairs and the head pastor Jud Wilhite walked down the hall. He saw me wandering around looking for something to do and said, "Excuse me, can I help you?" So I told him the same story: I'm a drug addict, I'm homeless, and I'd rather be here at the church. Jud said, "Well, nice to meet you, Cody. I'm Jud."

I said, "Yeah, I know, I've been watching you preach for the last couple of weeks, and I gotta tell you, there's some spiritual stuff going on in my life where I've been a really, really bad guy and now I feel like Jesus is calling me."

Jud said, "Well, you know, Cody, if Jesus is calling you, I suggest you answer the phone."

A few weeks later I was volunteering at the church and setting up rooms with table and chairs for a banquet. I went into a room and another volunteer started asking me questions. That was the beginning of my long friendship with Jack Dubanski.

Because I volunteered, the church didn't pay me for anything I did. But they let me have a free lunch from the cafeteria for working all day, which was cool. The cook knew that I was homeless. He had such a big heart – he always made me a sandwich that would take three days to eat. I'd tell him, "Man, I can't eat all this!" And he'd say, "Well, Cody, I got you some aluminum foil — why don't you eat what you can now and take the rest with you tonight for dinner?" I was like, "Man, thank you so much." I wasn't used to anyone being kind to me.

About a week later on a Sunday night after I'd been to church, I went back to the homeless park. My mind and my heart was full. I knelt near my oleander bush and wanted to pray. I didn't know how to pray. People at the church told me, "Cody, you just tell God what's on your heart."

So I did.

I leaned forward until my forehead reached the dirt and I said, "God, it's me, Cody. And you know what, Lord? I've been learning about what Jesus did on the cross, and about forgiveness and about mercy and about grace, and I understand that forgiveness is available to me. I've been driving my car my whole life and all I do is get into head-on accidents. Lord, if you'll have me, I would like you to drive my car, 'cause I'm tired of this life, I don't want to do this anymore. I can't do it. I have it all and I lose it all and I have it all and I lose it all, and I'm a drug addict. I need help."

Rivers of tears ran out of my eyes. I was on my knees in this dirt field, and just like the night at the dumpster, I cried so much that I made a mud puddle. But this time I said, "Lord, I accept You as my Father, and I pray that You will have Your way in my life."

I was sincere. I don't know how long I prayed. I spilled my heart out. I told God all the sins that I could remember about drugs and sex and violence and robbing and prison, and all of that stuff. I even added, "God, even for the sins that I committed against you that I don't even know or remember, I ask forgiveness. I ask you to be my Lord and Savior."

After I said, "Amen," I got up off my knees. The desire for drugs that I'd been fighting was totally gone. I just knew that I was no longer a drug addict. I'd used drugs the night before, and now I had no craving. Something happened inside of me. I truly believe the Holy Spirit came into me with such power that I was healed from all drug addiction at that very moment. I haven't touched any drugs or been tempted since.

When I stood up, all my thoughts were about Jesus: *Oh man, I gotta read my Bible, I gotta get in the Word, I need to pray more.* I could not get enough of the Word of God.

Other things changed immediately, too. Instead of thinking of myself as homeless, I started to think of myself as lucky. I convinced myself that I was on a camping trip. I didn't feel sorry for myself because I didn't have a home or anything else; it didn't matter to me. Along with those thoughts I felt joy in little things — like I didn't have bills to pay and that I didn't have to wake up early in the morning and go to work at a job I hated. I could be joyful that I was still alive.

Along with those changed inner thoughts, strange things happened in the park that first night.

About 40 other homeless people slept in the same field that I did. There is safety in numbers, so we formed an alliance. Sometimes we were bothered by robbers who came around and tried to steal our bicycles or food stamps – they knew who worked and who didn't. So we looked out for each other at night.

Although we had each other's backs, one thing that drug addicts and homeless people *don't* do is share their drugs. Homeless addicts get their drugs and go off by themselves to get high. They don't share anything, especially drugs. If you only have $20 to buy a rock it's better to smoke the whole $20 rock than it is to give somebody half of it. Drunks might share a bottle of beer or something, but drug addicts don't share because they have a monster to feed that lives inside. That's just the way it is.

When I said my prayer that night at the end of May, it was about 6:30. I was so full of joy it was very hard to go to sleep. But just when I'd start to doze off, someone woke me up and offered me dope. This had *never* happened before, and it happened all night.

"Hey Cody, here's some crack, man, I just put $10 on the pipe here," they'd say. That happened 'til like three in the morning. People woke me up five or six times trying to give me drugs.

I asked, "Where are you guys getting these drugs? Is somebody giving them away or what?" And they'd encourage me, "Oh never mind, Cody; here, take a hit." Finally, I had to stand up and threaten, "Man, the next person who wakes me up, we're gonna fight. I'm going to church in the morning and I don't care what you guys think about it — don't be offering me no more dope. I don't do dope anymore."

My best friend at the time, a guy named Steve, said, "Cody, what do you mean you don't do dope?" I said, "Man, I gave my heart to Jesus and He took away my craving for dope and I don't want it. You get that stuff away from me."

I understand now that it was spiritual warfare. The enemy saw me give my life to Christ and he pulled out all the stops to try and get me back. I read in Ephesians that we wrestle against principalities of darkness and that's exactly what happened. The enemy was trying to pull me back into the sin that I had been living in. But thank God, the very first scripture that I memorized during my Bible study time was Philippians 4:13: "I can do all things through Christ, who strengthens me."

I kept saying it over and over; it's such a simple verse to remember. I can do all things – circle in the Bible *all things*. That means that I can kick drugs, that means I can be a normal person again, that means I can get a job, which means I can do *all* things through Christ who strengthens me.

I just kept repeating that. That was the first verse that I memorized. I started thinking about that; *all things* doesn't mean *some* things.

The next day I went to church and I was so full. I don't know how else to describe it. This magical thing happened to me. I didn't feel sorry for myself anymore. I didn't feel like that homeless guy with no hope anymore. I didn't feel like, "I'm never gonna be normal again." I didn't feel like there's nothing I can ever do to get a job, or to get on my feet, or be normal; I didn't feel hopeless anymore.

Romans 8:31 describes perfectly how I felt. The Apostle Paul wrote, "If God be for us, who can be against us?" And I knew in my heart that now I had Jesus Christ in my life. I didn't know where the road was going to go, but I did know that God is for me. So nobody can be against me.

That day when I walked into church, I told people that I didn't even know, "Hey, my name's Cody, and guess what happened to me last night? I gave my heart to Jesus." They're like, "Oh, hallelujah! Let me pray for you!" Everything changed.

That was the day that people who worked at the church realized that I was serious about giving my heart to Christ. I had been there every day, and now I told anyone who'd listen that I'd been saved.

The church had a food pantry. The day after I got saved, someone took me down there when I was getting ready to leave for the night. The room was huge. It had everything. The guy told me to put whatever I wanted into my backpack because I'd been doing a lot of volunteer work around there for them and they wanted to make sure that I ate. He gave me a can opener too.

I filled my backpack with cans of Vienna sausages and spaghetti and whatever sounded good. I went back to the park and made gourmet meals like chili with Vienna sausages – all kinds of stuff. I could pull a feast out of that backpack, enough to feed myself and the three or four guys that I was most friendly with.

They did that for me every day. My church family did that for me *every* day. That was pretty cool. I felt loved.

CHAPTER 8

Taj Mahal, a Job, and a Heart Attack

I was baptized on June 23, 2004, about two weeks after my surrender to God near my oleander bush. I had just turned 53-years-old.

Before that happened, Central Christian required that I take an hour-long class. I learned about baptism and that it is an outward demonstration of an inward commitment. I understood that it is symbolic that the old self has gone and that I am a new man in Christ. I was so expectant of what God was going to do in my life; I knew there was going to be good things.

But I was nervous because of all the psychological problems that had developed in me during my childhood and when I was homeless and treated like a non-person. I mean, it wasn't that long ago that I let myself get horribly smelly because I didn't want a lot of interaction with anyone. Walking up in front of thousands of people to be baptized was intimidating.

But God sent Michelle – the woman who hugged me and told me that Jesus loves me. She came to my baptism and was the only person in the whole place that I knew.

Back in the dressing area where we were all getting ready with our baptism t-shirts, I really struggled with feeling nervous. All of a sudden there was a knock at the door and this guy poked his head in and asked, "Is there anybody in here named Cody?" I said, "I'm Cody!" He said that I had a visitor. Curious, I walked over to the door and there was Michelle.

I said, "Michelle, what are you doing here?" She said, "Are you kidding me? I wouldn't miss seeing you baptized for the whole world."

That made me feel so good. It was just what I needed. I knew that she had to go through a lot to be there; her husband didn't like her going to church every time there was something going on. So her coming to see me baptized was out of the box. I found out later that she flat put her foot down and said, "I'm going to see this homeless guy that I've been ministering to get baptized, and if you don't like it, I don't care. I'm going."

Mike, one of the pastors, baptized me – all the way under the water. When he pulled me back up, I had such joy and peace. I hugged Mike — there was a lot of cheering and applause. I felt like everything was going to be okay. I knew that I was a new man. I *felt* like this new creation — all the hurt and all the pain and all the condemnation and all that nasty stuff that I lived through my whole life was gone forever; it had been cast out to sea never to return.

I was full of such joy and I felt such energy and power that I didn't go to sleep that night. I was just too happy to get any sleep. I went back to the park and looked for people who were awake so that I could tell them about what just happened to me. And I was full of joy and peace and comfort and man – there is no high like the Most High. And believe me, I've tried them all; I'm an expert.

It's funny how word gets around in church even faster than it does in prison. People were talking about me and asking who I was because I was there every day. Most times people answered, "Well, he's a homeless guy and he just got saved and baptized and he's here every day and he wants to help."

One day — I remember this like it was yesterday — I was in the lunch room eating my monster sandwich. This guy walked up to me and said, "Hi, my name's Bob — you're Cody right?" I said, "Yes. Nice to meet you, sit down."

Bob sat down and looked me in the eyes and said, "Cody, how would you like to have a job?" I told him that I'd love to have a job. I didn't even ask what it was, how much it paid, if there were benefits or anything like that.

Bob said he thought he had a job for me and asked if I was ready. I went ballistic, "You're not kidding? A real job, a job where I would get paid?" He smiled and said, "Yeah, a job where you get paid." I was so excited I could hardly stand it when he asked if I was ready for more good news. He said, "A place to live comes with your job."

The job was at a place called Impact — a rock quarry. They wanted someone to work in the quarry during the day and be security at night for the equipment. Bob said I didn't really have to do anything at night, just that if I saw any cars pull in there to call the police. During the day I would work shoveling fallen gravel back onto conveyor belts.

I practically shouted, "Yes yes yes yes yes yes!"

Before I moved in to the little, 25-foot on-site travel trailer, two ladies, Irene and Kanani, put new curtains in it and scrubbed it all up. When I walked in there, it was like walking into the Taj Mahal. I had a place to stay. I had food in the cabinets, and not one bed, but two beds. I had a TV and a radio and a shower and toilet and a sink and a microwave. I was in seventh heaven.

Sometimes people who gave me rides home from church asked how I could live in that place all by myself. I always answered, "Man, I'm not all by myself, I got Jesus. How can I be alone if I have Jesus?" They found it hard to believe that I could live in a travel trailer in a rock crushing yard and be happy. I said, "What are you talking about? This is my castle. I have air conditioning, I have heating, I have a roof over my head, I have not one but two beds — I got it made. I got food in the icebox and in the cupboards. I'm rich."

When I started working there I was in bad shape. I was so skinny; I didn't have any muscle. All the hard work that I did, like throwing boulders around and shoveling sand was taxing my body. To tell you the truth, the first week that I was there, some of the guys took bets on how long I would last. But I reminded myself often, "I can do all things through Christ who strengthens me. I can do this. I can do it."

Two weeks after I was on the rock crusher, my body let me know it was having a hard time from the physical activity and not being on drugs for so long — and I was older – in my early 50s. I wasn't having any drug withdrawal symptoms, but I didn't feel quite right. One day I had really bad chest pain. Well, I'd eaten Mexican food the night before, so I thought it was indigestion.

All day long, all I could think was, *If I can make it home and lay down, I'll be okay.* I made it home, but it still felt like my heart was coming out of my chest. There wasn't anybody at the quarry by that time; they'd all gone home for the day. So I walked to a neighboring house. Thank God they were having a barbeque in their backyard. I asked them to call 911.

The ambulance took me to St. Rose. Sure enough, I was having a heart attack.

As soon as the hospital attendants put the EKG thing on, the doctor called a code on me. Because of my nursing background, I knew that particular code meant that I was gonna die. The crash team ran in with their cart. The doctor asked if I wanted a priest. I said, "No, I don't need a priest. I have Jesus. Could I just have a minute to pray?" He told me that I'd have to pray while he cut my chest open.

I prayed, "Lord, if this is my time to go, I'm ready. Let's go. Amen." That's all I said.

So help me, as soon as I said, "Amen," my heart went back to its normal sinus rhythm. Just like that. Everybody was shocked. The doctor finally managed to say, "I don't know what just happened."

I could see the astonished looks on everybody's faces. I looked at the doctor and told him that if he couldn't say Jesus, I certainly could. "I was just healed by Jesus!" I said.

The doctor finally said that was "all well and good," but they were going to leave the tube in my heart just in case anything happened. They put me into ICU so that they could keep an eye on me. RNs watched my monitor 24/7. Not once afterward did I have an irregular heartbeat.

From my nursing career I learned how to disconnect IVs and turn off machines. I got tired of sitting in bed. I decided that I wanted to go for a walk and unhooked myself. The RNs didn't like that much and chased me down the hall telling me that I was in critical condition and needed to get back in bed. I told them that I *wasn't* in critical condition but they could walk with me if they wanted to.

By then, Heather – the McDonald's Lady – and I had run into each other again through the church's ministry during a weekly Saturday barbecue that our church did in the homeless quarter. She said that she didn't remember me, but was thrilled that I'd been saved. After I got a job and she saw that I was really getting it and got baptized, she'd see me at church or the barbecue and hand me five or 10 McDonald's gift certificates at a time. She'd tell me, "Honey, I know you're working and I know you're having a rough time — so here."

Well, someone called the church to have them pray for me – then someone else who knew that Heather and I were friends called her and told her that I was dying and in critical condition at St. Rose.

Heather came running into my room in ICU and there I was, sitting up in bed like a happy camper. She wasn't overjoyed to see me perched there like I didn't have a care in the world. She said, "Cody, I could just whup on you! Someone called and told me you were dying!"

I grinned and told her, "I was, but I'm not dying anymore. I'm fine."

My doctor released me three days later. I have all the records from all of that. The doctors said that part of the reason the attack happened was because of the damage to my heart from being on cocaine for so long then coming off of it. I was totally healed.

After my discharge, I went back to the rock crusher job. The work was overwhelming and hard, and there were days where I had to carefully roll out of bed because my muscles hurt so bad. But one morning after I'd been there for a couple of months, I went into my bathroom to shave before work, and I looked in the mirror. I had muscles!

So I stayed on at the rock crusher and I made my $8 an hour. I knew I didn't have a big future there, but that was okay. I was happy.

After a church service one day, a guy named Scott came up to me where I was talking to people in the hallway. He shook my hand, introduced himself and asked what I knew about logistics. I told him that I go to my computer, put my credit card number in and stuff magically appears on my doorstep two or three days later. He laughed and said that I was exactly what he was looking for. He was aware of my criminal record, so that wasn't a problem. Scott offered me a job on behalf of UPS as a private contractor. My job was going to be getting freight in and out of shows in the city.

Scott said the problem that he always had with hiring logistics people is that they come into that aspect of the business and think they know everything. He wanted me to learn all of it from the ground up so that I could take over his job.

Las Vegas is the trade show capital of the world. Before the economy went south in 2007, there would be six or seven opening shows at different hotels and events across the city. My basic job for UPS was to organize all incoming freight and get it to the correct advance warehouse before the shows opened. Then I moved the freight into the shows to make sure they got to the right booths. I loaded one show in and went to another show. I also had to go around and see all the exhibitors to make sure that they were going to ship out with us.

The third phase of that job was loading out that show with the correct count on the exhibitors' bill. For example, I figured one 53-foot trailer for 10,000 pounds of freight. So I would total out how many trucks and how many trailers I needed. When the show closed, we loaded that show out and I gave my bills to waiting teamsters. Exhibitors spent tens of thousands of dollars at a time.

I was going to replace Tony, a guy who was relocating to Texas, so I trained under him two or three times a week. My employer at the rock crusher understood that it was a great opportunity for me – going from $8 to $25 an hour — so they gave me afternoons off in order to train on the UPS job.

That lasted for about two months. The extra income really helped because I needed to buy car insurance. Getting that car was one more way that God my Father provided for me: a few weeks earlier, I was waiting to be filmed for a success story clip at Central and tell my story about how I'd been saved and the impact that Jesus had on my life. I'd never met the guy I sat next to. He leaned over and said, "Your name is Cody, isn't it?" I told him it is, and he asked if I worked with the homeless. I said I did. He said, "You wouldn't know any homeless guy that needs a car, would you?" I told him, "Well I'm not homeless, but I'm in desperate need of a car because I have a job and I'm way out in the boondocks and I really have a problem getting to church and getting other stuff done."

He brought the car over and gave it to me a week later. Heather helped run me around to get insurance and all the things that I needed to be legal. I had wheels man. I was off to the rodeo.

Meanwhile, I still had issues with being around a lot of people — being talkative and friendly. My time with my mother and on the street left an unpleasant mark in me.

During the first month of my training, Tony took me to shows and conventions. There are a million people everywhere at those things. Tony introduced me to my future customers and I really had a problem there for a while. But I prayed for help; I asked God for strength, wisdom, energy and guidance to make it through those times and to not be nervous. Most of all, I wanted to come across as a God-fearing man, and that God would be glorified in everything that I did.

Before I knew it, I was a friendly guy and enjoyed taking care of my customers. It wasn't long before I went from being part-time to working 14 to 18-hour work days; I was able to leave the rock crusher job.

Sometimes we had to work at conventions that promoted the pornography industry. In Las Vegas — Sin City – there are a lot of sex-related events, including the adult video awards show. There was a porn show coming up, so Scott called to let me know I had the option to say, "No" because of my beliefs. I made a deal with him that I would do the show if I could invite my customers to church when I handed them my bill. I said I wouldn't beat anyone over the head with the Bible, though. He said, "Okay."

I did the show and I just tried to not look. There were a lot of half-naked people running around.

But that day turned out to be a really sweet thing, because of the types of people who are involved in the porn industry. Number one: they're very rich because they make a lot of money out of it. Number two: they're all unsaved or they wouldn't be doing the kind of business that they're doing. I found that when I invited them to church they thought it was a cool thing for a Christian man to do that. Funny thing is, a lot of people from those shows actually went to church the next time they were in town.

During that time, I learned that it's important to show the love of Christ living in us to *everyone*. Where would I be if Michelle hadn't hugged me? We may not come in contact with that person more than a minute. But in that minute, I'm going to show them pure, genuine love that comes from Christ, even if it's only that I bring Him up in conversation or I share something that I read in the Bible or an event that happened at church. He is the only one who will bring peace that passes understanding.

People who are lost see those qualities in us. It's an awesome thing. For people who live in sin, they see that love when you're nice to them; but they want to know what your motive is. There are a lot of sin-sniffers out there – those who try to sniff out people's sin and tell them how bad they are and that they're going to hell. Christians need to connect them into a relationship with Jesus Christ so they can find out what real love is.

Those on the outside need to understand that they have a Father who loves them and there's nothing so bad that He would love them any less, nor so good that He could love them any more than He already does. When people live burdened down by sin, they see that there's something different about you — like what I saw in Michelle and the way she looked at me. They naturally want to know more.

I'm living proof.

CHAPTER 9

She Said, "Yes"

For quite some time I'd volunteered with a church team that worked with homeless people on Saturdays down under the bridge by the Las Vegas Rescue Mission on Bonanza and D streets. It's called the homeless quarter and it's a really bad area.

Central Christian is a really large church, so we had a lot of helpers. We barbecued chicken and had all kinds of food to go with it. A lot of homeless people came out every week.

This is the place where I ran into Heather after the first few weeks that I'd been saved and baptized. I recognized her, walked up to her and said, "Excuse me, you may not remember me, but you gave me a McDonald's gift certificate a long time ago. Now I'm saved."

Heather didn't remember me. She said, "Honey, to tell you the truth, I give out so many of those things, I can't remember all the people that I give them to. But I'm really glad you're saved." We became true friends.

As I mentioned before, Heather still gave me McDonald's gift certificates when she saw me at church or the homeless outreaches. After I'd been working at the rock crusher a while, I was on my feet and saving money and I didn't need them any longer. One day she handed a few more to me. I nicely told her, "Heather, give those to somebody else. I don't need those anymore." Well, she was thrown back because anyone else in my situation would've taken them. But I explained that I was saving my money and had groceries now and didn't really need them; give them to somebody who does. It blew her away, because she never had that happen before.

At the time that I met Heather, she was 62 and working full-time at a photography studio. She had retired from working at The Rio hotel and casino and lived alone in her house; she volunteered at the homeless outreach in her spare time. She kept McDonald's gift certificates in her purse and handed them out at as she drove around the city.

Heather grew up in a functional, loving family in Canada. She was really good in school and sports. She played basketball, volleyball, grass hockey and she was in drama club. After high school, she moved to the United States and went to Logan Chiropractic College in St. Louis, Missouri. By then she was married and had two children: Nathan who was born in 1962 and Suzanne born in 1964. Heather also graduated in 1964 and went on to be a successful Chiropractic doctor for two years. After she gave birth to Victoria in 1965, she decided to be a full-time, stay-at-home mom.

Heather's marriage ended in divorce in 1972. Her mother was ill, so Heather decided to move to Las Vegas where her parents had moved in the 1960s.

Although Heather had grown up "in the faith" she fell away from walking with the Lord during her first marriage. However, her sister and daughter Suzie love the Lord and encouraged her to come back to church with them – at Central Christian. She started going there about 1999 or 2000.

After I had that heart attack, Heather stepped up to help me with shopping and laundry and doing errands; she took me to classes at church in the evenings four nights a week after I'd worked on the rock crusher all day. All I could give her in return was gas money and my gratitude.

On one particular day, Heather drove me back to my trailer. We were heading south on Eastern at the part where it goes under 215. To this day, I remember exactly where it was; I looked over at her and she just looked different to me. We'd been friends for about a year and she looked different; she looked attractive. I hadn't noticed that before because we were just friends. But all of a sudden, Heather made my heart go pitter-patter — I felt like it was going to leap out of my chest and I was like... WOW.

So I sat there in her car with all kinds of emotions going through me. Several months earlier I knew that somehow, some way I needed a woman in my life. I was a young guy in my early 50s, man. And I just gave it all to God. And I asked God only once, "Lord, you know that I'm going to need a companion. I know that you have the perfect woman already picked out for me." And I left it at that.

So that night after I saw Heather differently I had a dream that Heather and I were married. When I woke up, I was like, *Whoa, this is weird.*

From that point forward I had warm and fuzzy emotions about her. The more Heather and I were around each other, which was four or five times a week, the more my feelings grew. I finally couldn't stand it anymore; I had to talk to her. At the time I was still working for UPS and the rock crusher.

I thought about all of the time that she had sacrificed to help me — giving me rides, shopping, helping me to get on my feet after I was in the hospital and until I got a car. My feelings toward her were growing deeper roots.

The funny thing is that despite the time we spent together, we'd never spoken too much about intimate details of our lives. I didn't know what she would think about how my feelings toward her were developing. What if this woman had already made up her mind that she was happy being single for the rest of her life?

So I prayed and prayed and after a few weeks felt the Holy Spirit nudging me to go and talk to her. By this time I had my own car. I drove down to where Heather worked at the photography studio down in the Rio area. It was a long drive from the rock crusher. It felt extra-long that day.

Man, I had sweaty palms. I was so nervous. All the way down there I had conversations in my head: *What if I tell Heather this? What if she says that? How will I respond? What will I say?* Finally, I just prayed, "Lord I need your help. I need your guidance in this situation."

When I pulled up and parked in front of the building where she worked, her boss walked out of the office, got in his car and left. It was about two o'clock in the afternoon. So that meant Heather and I were there all alone.

As I walked up to the building, I was prepared for rejection and I kept praying. It seemed as if the Holy Spirit was leading me to just confess my feelings for her. So I saw her and words just came out of my mouth – and they were nothing like what I had thought about that I would say. The words came out like this: "Heather, I don't know how to put this into words but my feelings toward you are beginning to change." I looked her in her eyes and said, "Heather, I think I'm falling in love with you." That was the hardest thing I've ever said.

Her response floored me. Heather smiled and said, "Cody, I'm so glad you came over here, because I've wanted to talk to you about this." I walked around her desk and she stood up and I gave her a hug and we had our first kiss. I remember it like it was yesterday. She was just like, "Oh Cody this is so cool because I've been praying about this." And I said, "Well so have I!" It felt like this big burden was lifted off of my shoulders.

I can honestly tell you, I don't think either one of us had any thoughts during that first year of our friendship that we would ever date or fall in love.

That night we talked on the phone for three hours. We didn't go out on a date then because I had to go to work the next day, but we started to officially date and go out to dinner and hang out more as friends – not just doing errands.

It was funny, all of a sudden when Heather and I went shopping it was a different — it was like a date. We were falling in love. I found myself calling her and talking on the phone for an hour or two every day. I'd say, "Heather, you know, if you're busy…" and she'd say, "No, no, I'm not busy, let's talk."

After about a year of getting to know each other, I decided to ask her to marry me.

I called Heather at home – it was January 2005 — and asked if I could come by because there was something on my heart that I need to talk to her about. She said that would be fine.

When I got there I went into the front room where she was. I got down on my knees and said, "I didn't know what love was until I met you. Heather, I love you more than anything in the whole world. And I just wanna ask you to marry me because I love you so much."

She said, "Yes" immediately.

I was so happy at that moment. I couldn't even believe that she wanted to marry me too. I realized later that she obviously had been thinking and praying about it and probably knew it was coming but didn't know when.

I wish it could've been romantic and that I had more money to make it extravagant. But I just got down on my knees and asked. She said, "Yes." And I was a happy camper.

When I asked Heather to marry me, God really put it on my heart to tell her everything — *everything*. Don't hide anything, tell her everything. I didn't want this wonderful woman to marry me without knowing my whole story. Heather knew about some of the stuff in my past, but not all the dirty, nitty-gritty parts.

After I proposed, I told her that we needed to have meetings together so that I could go over my previous life with her. She kept telling me that it didn't matter. But it was important to me. I didn't want her to hear something later from someone else and have to say, "Hey Cody, you never told me about that. I didn't know that."

It took me about 10 days to tell her everything; an hour here, two hours there. All along she kept telling me it didn't matter, she knew that I am a new man in Christ. But I wanted her to know; I *needed* her to know. A friend later joked with me that I confessed in 10 minutes to God, but Heather took 10 days.

We set the date for April 2, 2005 – four months later. Telling her family was a real concern. I was out of touch with mine then, so we didn't need to worry about that. But we had to get her son, her two daughters and her sister together and tell them that she was going to marry me.

When we told them, they thought we were setting an April Fool's joke. They didn't really take it too good.

Heather's children knew that the Cody their mom was friends with had come from "the other side." I'd met them before at a few family parties, but it was always as Heather's friend from church whom she helped out. They truly wondered if she'd gone crazy, if she needed to be committed, she didn't have to *marry* this guy.

Truthfully, if the tables were turned and someone that I loved was going to marry a guy with my kind of past, I would have been definitely against it until I saw his transformation for myself. They knew who I was, but they didn't *know* me. I understood their concerns. There I was, wanting to marry their mother, their sister. They didn't know if I would have a good income or a good future; they were skeptical for a long time, even after we married.

But Tori, Heather's youngest daughter, calls me Dad. Her heart sang when she found out we were getting married – she was so happy for us. It took a while for the others to come around. Tori won a place in my heart that day. She said, "This is so cool that somebody like you guys can fall in love and be so happy." She just won my heart, she really did.

We arranged for Pastor Bill Nordstrom from Central to perform the ceremony in a gazebo in Heather's sister's back yard in Vegas. Everything was decorated. There was a swimming pool with candles and flowers floating in it, and paper ribbons everywhere. The gazebo where we exchanged vows looked like the Ark of the Covenant or something. I had developed a lot of friendships at church but I was unprepared for how many were at our wedding. When I walked into that backyard – wow. A lot of people were there. The women were dressed up like the Taj Mahal. It was beautiful. Beautiful.

Now that we've been together a lot of years, Heather's large family are my friends. They are totally on my side now. Heather's son, Nathan, and I are very good friends; I get along with the whole family. In 2015 we celebrated our 10-year anniversary.

We joke now – I tell people, "I'm not stupid, I married the McDonald's Lady."

Cody and Heather's wedding.

Food line supplies.

Food prep.

Outreach team.

Left: Jerry, one of our volunteers at the Christmas event with Pastor Cody.

Below: People lining up for food at our Christmas event.

Cody's many mugshots.

Pastor Cody at the park.

Cheryl, Lee, Heather, and Cody at Woodlands Church in Texas.

Cody and Uncle Glen's final picture.

CHAPTER 10

Coming Full Circle with Uncle Glen

While I was making good money at UPS, I bought myself another Harley. I'd had them before, but always lost them because I had to feed the monster living inside of me.

Heather and I were on a motorcycle trip one day, coming back home to Las Vegas. A friend – I call him my nephew – was in a magic show in Arizona so Heather and I made it a road trip with a stop at the Hoover Dam. It was a fairly long ride.

Heather playfully thumped me on the back of my helmet, leaned forward and teased, "You always drive one mile up the road and one mile back."

Of course, she knew about Uncle Glen and the special times I had with him — how he was my childhood hero, how much I still loved him, and that he is the one who taught me to ride. We finally stopped at the Dam, and Heather started in on me, "Cody, you gotta call your uncle Glen." She just kept on me into the next day. She wouldn't let up. It took persuading, because I didn't think that he would want to hear from me. And I didn't know his phone number anymore — it had been 30 years.

So that next day I called information in Klamath Falls, Oregon, got his information and dialed. He answered the phone. I was totally surprised when he started to cry. All the family that was left up there thought I had been dead for 30 years because I had disappeared. He was so glad to hear my voice.

As soon as I was able, I rode up to Klamath Falls on my Harley for a visit. When I arrived, 75-year-old Uncle Glen came out of his house, looked at my bike and said, "You really took this seriously." I told him, "Well, yeah Uncle Glen. You taught me. I've been riding motorcycles all my life." I took him for a ride.

On that first visit I had a wonderful time with Uncle Glen and the rest of my family. By then, my mom had been dead for about 10 years. I went up again three more times just to hang out and spend time with him. We worked in the garage on his motor home and did things together that we used to do when I was a kid.

Those four trips were times of healing and a chance for me to tell him how much he meant to me. I told him that I was so sorry for not reaching out during all of those years that had gone by. I mean, it had been 30 years since the last time I saw him. I had been too ashamed of what he'd think of me.

Those visits were wonderful. Me and my uncle prayed together and I reconnected with my family – cousins and aunts and uncles. They were thrilled that I was still alive and a Christian. I mean they were *totally* thrilled.

By my third visit, Uncle Glen had been diagnosed with brain cancer. I visited him twice more when he was sick; the last time was an emergency. He was nearing the stage where he would be comatose so the family called to tell me that I didn't have much time to get there before that happened. They brought him home into Home Hospice care.

I got in the Mustang and I'll tell you what — I had the pedal to the metal. I got stopped twice; once was at 3:30 on the morning that I left Vegas. I was doing about 90 and the Highway Patrol pulled me over. The officer said, "Sir, you're going way too fast. Have you had anything to drink tonight?" I said, "No, I'm stone cold sober. My uncle is dying in Oregon and I'm trying to get to him before he dies." The cop said, "Sir, I don't even need to see your license or anything. Just slow it down. You're going to make it." I said, "Man. Hallelujah."

So I got back on the road and kept driving above the speed limit. I'm not going to lie to you. I just had to get there before my uncle passed away. I just had to get there. When I was about 30 miles outside of Klamath Falls, I focused on how close I was getting to my uncle's bedside. I pushed the Mustang and hauled through the desert. I mean I just hauled. I came up over this little hill and there sat a Highway Patrol. I was doing 102.

I just pulled over to the side of the road. I knew he had me. I didn't even wait for him to make a U-turn or flash his lights. I just pulled over. He probably noticed my license plate frame that asked, "What Would Jesus Do Next?" I wasn't a very good witness, I knew. I explained the story to him, and he let me go. He said, "Well, you better hurry up and get there." He didn't write me a ticket.

So I went the speed limit going into Klamath Falls and I got there in plenty of time because Uncle Glen didn't pass until about four days later.

During those last days with him I was like a puppy dog. I stayed by his side. I read the Bible to him. I prayed. I ministered to him and he accepted Jesus Christ as his personal Lord and Savior.

Three days before he died, he went into a total coma. But during my nursing career I was always taught that even though somebody is in a coma they can still hear you.

So I told him stories about the memories I had with him from when I was a kid and we water-skied, rode motorcycles and played baseball. We used to have so much fun. Some of my favorite memories are occasions spent at different lakes camping out for a week, having barbecues and water-skiing. I talked to Uncle Glen about happy stuff. And I read the Bible to him a lot.

My aunt – my mother's sister — had passed away many years before. Uncle Glen had remarried a Christian lady. That was cool. My new aunt and I stood next to his bed and prayed. It was the sweetest time.

During his last moments, I held Uncle Glen in my arms and recited the 23rd Psalm. His eyes were already closed and his breathing had the death rattle. The whole family – about 20 people – were there and we all knew he was going to pass at any minute. He took one final, deep breath and then he was gone.

I turned to the family with tears running down my face, and someone said, "Is Dad okay?" I said, "No, he's gone." But it was such an honor. I mean, yeah I cried and I hurt and all of that stuff — but that's just my selfishness. The way that I think about that man; he went out of his way so many times for me. It was my honor to be there when he took his last breath on Earth. I spent a lot of time thanking God for Heather, too. God used her to force me to call my uncle.

In those moments after Uncle Glen passed, we all prayed that peace and understanding would rule our hearts. We knew that Uncle Glen had already accepted Christ. We knew that he was in no more pain, no more agony. He was with Jesus.

Then there was a little bit of scurry – one final act of love I wanted to do for Uncle Glen was to get him presentable and ready for the mortuary. When people go, they often make a "mess" so I had to get the family away and out of the room in order to get him cleaned up and dressed before they arrived in a few minutes to take him away. While he was able, Uncle Glen had picked out what he wanted to wear.

I had planned to stay for his ceremony. He spent a lot of time in the Navy, so there was a naval burial planned with a 21-gun salute and all of the bells and whistles. But it seemed that it wasn't long after he took his last breath that the family put locks on his garage. He had so many tools and people started talking about, "Well that car is mine," arguing about who got what – the fighting started.

I went outside. He had a motorhome, so I went into it and prayed. It seemed that God clearly told me, "Your job is done here." I went back inside where the family was and I told them my heart, "You know, this is ridiculous. Uncle Glen isn't even cold yet and you guys are putting padlocks on stuff and saying, 'This is mine.' I can't be around this. I gotta go."

So I left. I couldn't handle it. I'm talking an hour after my uncle had taken his last breath — fighting over his toys, his motorcycles and his motorhome and all of his stuff. I didn't want to be in the middle of that. I didn't want family arguments to rule my last memories about my uncle.

I jumped in the Mustang and drove home. I cried a lot. I called some of my friends — Jack Dubanski was one of them. I phoned him, but a lot of the calls were just me crying. I mean, I couldn't really talk. Jack just listened and said, "Well Cody. You know what? He's in a better place now. He's with Jesus. And that's where we all want to be."

Klamath Falls is about five hours north of Reno if you're going the speed limit. And I did. By the time I got to Reno, I had pretty much settled down. I started to feel blessed that I was able to be there with my hero. I decided to focus on thanking God.

The time surrounding Uncle Glen's death was also a big testament to the complete work that God has done in me.

If this had happened during my earlier years — the great joy of being restored to my uncle only to have him taken from me in death such a short time later and to see the family in-fighting over "stuff" — I would have gone into an emotional tailspin and back to my "friends."

But I didn't even think of escaping into drugs. It didn't cross my mind.

This time I ran straight into my Father's presence.

CHAPTER 11

The Calling Just Got Stronger

After Heather and I married, we focused on daily helping the city's homeless in addition to volunteering with the weekly church outreach program.

Between the two of us, we bought $500 worth of McDonald's gift certificates at a time and went through a lot of our own money fast to get other supplies. God touched our hearts for these people and we wanted to help them.

Heather was still working at the photography studio and by this time I was working up to 18-hours a day as a private freight contractor for UPS.

During our trips out and about the city, we saw destitute people standing on corners holding signs, or some of our own homeless guys that we knew, and gave them five Mc-

Donald's certificates at a time. They were perfect to give because those things are very hard to sell. The homeless couldn't really sell them or trade them in exchange for beer or drugs because people didn't know if they were any good. It looked like funny money and in those days, people didn't even know McDonald's offered gift certificates.

We did this every day. When the weather got colder, we went down to the old JC Park which is now Justice Myron E. Leavitt and Jaycee Community Park to hand out blankets and make sure that everyone was warm and had what they needed. The weather starts to turn pretty cold in Las Vegas around the end of October. When you're used to overnight temperatures in the 80s all summer, 50-something degrees can feel pretty cold. By December and January, the temperature can drop into the 30s overnight.

About six months after our wedding, Heather was shopping at the Albertson's grocery store a few blocks from our house. This is the exact same Albertson's parking lot where I first met Heather and asked if I could wash the windshield on her car and she said, "No," but gave me McDonald's instead. In fact, I went up to the manager a few years ago and said, "Do you remember when you used to kick me out of your parking lot?" He just got a blank look, as if to say, *What? We never used to kick you out of our parking lot.*

Anyway, Heather was shopping for vegetables and got to talking to the produce manager. Heather told the lady what we do with the homeless community. In a flash of inspiration, Heather asked what happens to all the food coming up for expiration and produce that is getting old. The woman took Heather to see the store manager who said, "Lady, if you want that stuff, you can have it." They told her to come by every day and take whatever they had.

Starting the next morning, Heather and I got up real early, went to Albertson's and loaded both of our cars with food and took it to the park. We did that every day. Oh, you wouldn't believe the food we got. The manager let us have all their expiring deli stuff, all their fruit, and all their vegetables, all of their pastries. We even got stuff like hamburgers and pork chops. Oh man, we had more food than we knew what to do with.

Our homeless friends knew that we would be at the park every day. The park is redone now, but at that time the picnic tables were close together. We purchased pots so they could make stews, and we bought frying pans and spatulas and utensils. They ate like kings. We had the fattest homeless community in Las Vegas.

We did that for about a year until someone sued Albertson's over a homeless guy who took something to eat out of a garbage can and got sick. He wasn't from our park. He won a settlement. So Albertson's came up with a rule that only refrigerated trucks were allowed to pick up food from their store. So there went a huge source of food because, of course, we didn't have a refrigerated truck.

When that ended in 2005, Heather and I still had all these people that we loved out there who needed somebody to look after them, so we began to fund out of our pockets whatever they needed. We still carried McDonald's gift certificates with us wherever we went. Now we added food bags that we'd make up at home and carry them around to hand out to whoever needed them. When we saw someone on the street, sometimes we pulled over to pray with them and see how they were doing. If they needed to go to the doctor, we took them. When we could, we'd host meals in parks.

Shortly after Heather and I started feeding the homeless community in the park with Albertson's leftovers, we were invited to spend our first Christmas dinner at a family party. They asked us to bring a turkey. While it was thawing out a few days in advance, they called and said they didn't need the turkey after all.

So Heather and I came up with an idea, and I know it was straight from God. We cooked the turkey anyway, made all the trimmings for a Christmas dinner, went to Marie Calendar's and bought pies, and went to the park on Christmas morning. We unloaded our car onto a picnic table. There were 12 homeless people sitting there in the park.

I knew their hearts had to be broke. I know, because I had been out there at Christmas. Being homeless, you think about all the times in the past that you spent with loved ones, and you think about all those Christmases. And here you are, homeless and in a park on Christmas Day. It's a horrible, horrible feeling.

Anyway, Heather and I got out of the car – nobody knew we were coming. We walked up with a cooked turkey and pies, and mashed potatoes and gravy and everything. They looked at us and one said, "What are you guys doing?" I said, "Well, we know that you guys didn't have anywhere to go for Christmas, so we brought you Christmas dinner." Everybody started crying.

We stayed with them for five or six hours and we just had a blast. When Heather and I got back into our car to go to our family dinner that we were invited to, we looked at each other and simultaneously said, "I don't want to spend Christmas any other way than serving people."

The year turned into 2006 and another glitch happened that made it harder for us to feed people.

That summer the Las Vegas city council passed a law that forbade feeding the homeless in city parks. Violating the ordinance was a misdemeanor to be punished by a fine of up to $1,000 or a jail term of up to six months — or both. The ordinance was reportedly in response to public complaints about the homeless frightening residents and making the parks ugly.

Well, I came home from work a little early one day and the news was on. The headline was, "It is now illegal to feed homeless people in Clark County." I looked at Heather and was like, "What? I'm not going for this!" Heather looked at me and said, "Well, Cody, what are you going to do?" I said, "I'm going to get an attorney and I'm going to sue the city!" Just like that. I didn't have to think about it, I didn't have to pray about it, I didn't have to anything. This was not right.

Because we had been feeding the homeless and taking care of them, it was like a lightning bolt hit me. The next day, I got an attorney and I found five like-minded individuals who ran ministries or fed people, and we filed a lawsuit. We sued the mayor. We sued the United States marshals. We sued the metropolitan police. We sued the city council. We sued everybody we could sue. The case ended up in Federal Court. Our attorney told us going in, "Hey guys, don't be surprised if we lose this case because this judge is not very lenient toward homeless issues."

Before we went into the courtroom, the five of us prayed. The mayor was confident and surrounded by his five attorneys. In fact, he was an attorney.

I'll never forget that day or what the Federal judge who heard the case said. The judge looked at the mayor and his attorneys and basically said, "Do you guys realize that if I were to let you get away with infringing on civil rights like this, not only is this against the law, it's against the Constitution of the United States? So if I let you make a law targeting a certain group of people, what's to keep you from making laws that target black people, or Mexican people, or purple people, or yellow people? I cannot allow this. This is unconstitutional." He ruled in our favor and also awarded us attorney's fees.

We were national news; it went all across the country because other cities were planning on trying to do what Las Vegas city council did. The prevailing attitude seemed to be, *Stop feeding stray animals and they'll stop coming around.* But because we won, nobody else in the entire country came up with anything.

During this issue, we didn't know how much longer we could keep feeding our homeless community by ourselves. Heather had retired that year after she turned 65 and started drawing off her Social Security. We started to run low on money despite the big checks that I got from UPS every two weeks.

I hadn't worked at the rock crusher for a long time and had been exclusively with UPS for about five years. My two-week paycheck was usually $5,000 or $6,000. But that job was such a monster. If I was married to anyone but Heather I would be divorced right now because there isn't a woman in the world that would put up with their husband working 16 to 18-hour days and coming home all burnt out. When I got home, all I wanted was something to eat and to go to bed for six hours, then get up in the morning and do it all over again.

Although I was exhausted from working such grueling hours, I was finally at a good place in my life. My relationship with Jesus was first and foremost, then my relationship with my wife, and then my job with UPS.

But on my way to work, I'd stop for gas and see the homeless people in the park. They were all friends of mine. I couldn't get them out of my heart. I felt so sorry for them. Even though Heather and I always carried McDonald's or homemade food bags around to hand out, it just didn't seem like it was enough.

During this time I went down to the Salvation Army to help with an outreach. A three-year-old girl, the cutest thing I ever saw, walked up to me and said, "Hi." Well, I love kids, and I said "Hi Honey, how are you?" She had the biggest, most beautiful brown eyes. She said, "I'm fine." I didn't see any adults around who looked like they were taking care of her, so I asked her if I could pick her up and find where she belonged. When I took her in my arms, boy, she put her arms around me and wasn't about to let go. She had the attitude, *Wherever you're going, I'm going.*

I asked her, "Honey, what are you doing here? Are you helping with the outreach?" She said, "No, I live here, me and my mama and my brothers and sisters." I asked where they were and she pointed to a lady who was sitting on a low brick wall surrounded by four other kids – ages five, eight, 10 and 13. I walked up to her, holding her child in my arms, and I told her that her baby girl is beautiful. That led to a bit of conversation and finally I asked, "How did you get out here?"

Her name is Kim, and she told me that her boyfriend left her, took all the money and left her homeless with five children; she had nowhere to go and had to hang out at the Salvation Army. I asked if anyone was helping her and she said, "No." I couldn't believe it. All those church people who came down there and nobody's helping her at all — not doing anything for her. She said, "They tell me that they'll pray for me." I was mad. "Pray for you? That's not enough to pray for you! Somebody needs to be doing something for you!" I said the words that God put on my heart.

I remember that day so vividly. I rode home on the freeway on my motorcycle all the way from the Salvation Army and cried like a baby because it broke my heart that this lady was down there with five kids. It just broke my heart. When I walked into the house I was still crying. Heather came up and put her arms around me and said, "Honey, what's wrong?" I told her the story, and she put her foot down and said, "Well, we gotta do something about this."

What happened next is God — I never pat myself on the back, I pat God on the back — God put it on my heart to help this lady, so we did a fund drive. We went on Facebook and told our friends and family and anybody who would be willing to help in any way. We took pictures of Kim and her children and carried them around with us. We told people that we ran into about them.

We raised $15,000. So we rented a place for them to stay for six months, furnished it, and gave her everything that she needed to get on her feet. Now she had a place where she could get cleaned up and look for a job; she got one at a casino in North Las Vegas. We didn't have to urge her to do that – she was ready and just needed a hand up. She ran into another lady who was having a problem finding a place to stay so they made a deal – Kim let her come over and watch the kids while she went to work.

And Kim got saved, which is best of all. But that one was huge — to go to bed at night and know that those children had beds to sleep in and food in their bellies and didn't have to sleep on a corner at the Salvation Army with all the crackheads and drug addicts and everybody else running around.

We have stayed in touch. Today, eight years later, she's still doing really good. She's still working, she's falling in love and has a car and all that she needs.

Helping Kim and her kids out wasn't a big thing for Heather and me and it wasn't a big thing for God – we were available to be used by Him. We wanted more of that.

That calling was continuously on our hearts. We couldn't get the homeless community off of our minds. When it was summertime and really hot, we bought cases of water bottles to hand out and did whatever else we could find to do. In the wintertime when it was raining outside, we'd sit at home or in our car and cry and wonder where everybody was keeping dry. We prayed that God would provide somebody to bring them food, because when the weather turns bad like that they hide in tunnels and all over the place, so we never exactly knew where they were.

The calling just got stronger that God wanted us to work with them. The more we talked about it, the more it increased. I worked really long hours but we tried in our own way to help as much as we could, and we couldn't get them off our hearts or minds.

We were so busy that sometimes my pockets were full of hundred dollar bills but I didn't have time to spend any of it on supplies. I knew better than to hand out cash to any of the homeless; it would go straight into a bottle, a pipe, a vein, gambling, or up their noses. So Heather and I put it into food and doctor visits and whatever else we could think of.

You know, I understand that homeless people have made mistakes. But I don't think that somebody should have to pay for a mistake for the rest of their lives. We were out there trying to give them a hand up, not a handout.

I knew the Holy Spirit was stirring in me to do more. But I couldn't figure out how to make it work.

Six years before, when I left my oleander bush to move into my Taj Mahal-like trailer and got steady work at the rock crusher, all of my homeless friends at the park said, "Well, Cody got a job and Cody got a place to live and we're never gonna see Cody again." I always replied with, "Hey, you guys are still gonna see me." I knew then that I would not abandon them.

Truthfully, I just didn't know how. In my mind, I was still gonna stop by and check on them and give them McDonald's or whatever I could as I got on my feet. Now I had a better paying job and a savings account, but that didn't make me happy. I worked long hours, but it wasn't what I thought God wanted me to do anymore. And the money was getting used up pretty fast.

I thought back to something that happened during my last days as a homeless man in the park: when one of them leaves because they got a job or moved away or got a place to live, their homeless friends throw a party.

That means cooking whatever they can come up with. It's their way of pooling what little resources they have as a show of friendship and support in order to say, "Goodbye and good luck."

In *their* minds, their "goodbye" to me in 2003 was final. It wasn't. God had other plans.

PART 3

CHAPTER 12

The Beginning of Broken Chains

Slowly but surely the stirring for change increased in our hearts; I was certain by now that God was calling Heather and me into full-time ministry. The more we prayed about it, the stronger we felt the Spirit nudging both of us to trust Him and go out to work full-time with the homeless community.

We'd been doing it on our own for five years in between working hours and on weekends. At that time we fed them, gave them things they needed and prayed with them, but we weren't doing sermons and Bible studies like we do now.

It was also getting to a point that we didn't know if we could afford it anymore. But something would always happen; people from church heard that we worked with the homeless and they kept us going. The phone would ring and someone on the other end would say that they wanted to help us. They had food, clothing, and lots of different things. We knew that it was God stepping in and touching people's hearts to help us.

We sought outside counsel from people whom we trusted about becoming non-profit and going full-time. We prayed about it for 30 days. We talked about what this plan would look like if I didn't have an income from UPS and drew on my Social Security and Heather's too.

Heather's family thought we were nuts. "There's no money in a homeless ministry," they said, "have you lost your minds? You're not going to have any money." They didn't know how we were going to survive.

But we knew that the Bible tells us God will provide. Philippians 4:19 says that our God will supply all of our needs according to his riches in glory in Christ Jesus.

We came up with a plan to pay off our house and all of our bills and live off our combined Social Security. We trusted God for the rest. So we stood on the Word of God and the faith that He gave us, and we didn't listen to what people said about there not being money in that particular ministry.

The biggest reason we didn't listen to that argument is because we weren't doing it to *make* any money. Heather and I are interested in souls for the Kingdom of God. We were interested in if our people had something to eat, if they were cool in the summertime and warm in the wintertime. *That's* what motivated us.

We started attending Hope Baptist Church in 2007 and decided to go into full-time ministry in the later part of 2008. I had to get paperwork started to create a 501(c)

(3) for our ministry that we named Broken Chains to be a non-profit corporation; there were 45 pages of government documents. There were so many questions. It was returned three times for more information, but eight months later we received approval.

Meanwhile, I worked until we paid off all of our bills: our home, our cars, my motorcycle, everything except the normal monthly bills that come in. We wanted to start in ministry without any debt.

I also started counseling sessions at Hope with Pastor Vance Pittman and began the ordination process so that I could become a pastor. Pastor Vance gave me a stack of books that was four-feet high and told me to read them all. Today he jokes that he put me under a spotlight and withheld food and water until I answered all the questions right.

By the time we got our 501(c)(3) I had already quit my job and I had to do all of these studies and tests to be ordained, and it was really a lot.

The ordination process is learning about all the things that have to do with being in ministry. I had meetings with Pastor Vance and some of our other pastors. We talked about the calling of God and they asked me questions. They'd never been involved with a homeless ministry. So they asked questions like, "Cody, how are you going to do...?" whatever. I told them that I'm going to trust God.

I studied every day and had to write papers. I needed to be able to serve communion, perform baptisms and weddings, and stuff like that. I thank God that I had been attending Thursday Morning Bible Study (TMBS) in Las Vegas on a regular basis for many years, so I already had a really good, sound understanding of theology. But man, those books that the church gave me. Every day was a learning process. It was a whole lot of study and a lot of prayer. It was like a Jesus Boot Camp.

I was hauling along and doing really, really good, and then I hit the brakes and screeched to a halt; I came to this question: "Why do bad things happen to good people?" I asked the Lord to help me answer it. I just didn't know. And I didn't want to give a butterfly answer with Romans 8:28 which encourages us that all things work together for good. The more I prayed about it, the more I searched my heart.

When I told Pastor Vance my answer, he said that I couldn't have put it any better. My answer was, "I don't know."

I would have a hard time believing anyone who came up with a philosophical answer. That question goes really, really deep and only God can answer it. I'm not going to pretend that I have an answer.

So anyway, after I was ordained and Broken Chains was given non-profit status, we put the word out that we were officially started in ministry and planned to hold an outreach at the same park where I had been homeless. To tell you the truth, we didn't have any money to fund it. We didn't know how many people were gonna show up, and we didn't know what kind of food we were gonna serve. So we prayed.

Three days before that first outreach, the Las Vegas Rescue Mission people called and told us to come down and get whatever we needed for our outreaches. They've been our partner in ministry now for six years; they supply about 80 percent of the food that we serve.

So we went down there and they gave us a 40-pound box of cut-up chicken to barbecue — which was more than enough. They gave us barbecue sauce, fruit and vegetables, and bread. They even gave us paper plates, forks, spoons, napkins and other things we didn't have.

Our first outreach went really, really well. Everybody had a blast. We did a sermon and it went really good and everybody had fun. Heather and I were happy because it was our joy to bring such joy to those people. We've also turned the outreach into a place where it's not just feeding them; they know that if anyone wants prayer we will be more than happy to pray for them.

When it was over and we were cleaning up, Heather and I said to each other, "We need to keep doing this."

There were challenges of course as we did more outreaches — we work with the "least of these:" drug addicts, alcoholics, prostitutes, and crazy people. But it was our joy to be down there and feed them all and to minister the Word of God – to let them know about the grace and love and forgiveness and mercy that are available to them in Christ. It was, and still is, an honor.

Even before we were officially a nonprofit, people from our new church home at Hope heard that we worked with the homeless and funded our outreach to them out of our own pockets. All of a sudden our phone started ringing with offers of help and food and clothes and other things. That was God stepping in; we were at a place where we didn't know how much longer we were going to be able to continue the ministry by using our own money.

God answered our prayers in every way. That was just the beginning.

CHAPTER 13

A Harley Christmas to All

Over the following weeks and months while Heather and I stood on Philippians 4:19, we saw that God really does provide according to His riches in glory in Christ Jesus. God owns everything. Broken Chains is not something that Heather and I built – it is what God has done.

As our ministry has grown, I've only solicited one company for sponsorship. The people who work at Las Vegas Harley Davidson know me because I've bought my brand-new bikes from them over the span of 15 years – before and after drug addiction. I purchased my Deuce, Softail and a Road King.

When I asked if they would sponsor us by letting us use their parking lot for a Christmas event, they said, "Yes!" immediately.

That first Christmas that Heather and I shared with 12 homeless people grew into a massive party over the course of eight years. Harley Davidson partnered with us and it grew bigger every year. At our last big one in 2012 we had 1,400 homeless people and about 600 volunteers.

During those Christmas parties we provided a complete turkey dinner with all the trimmings, and gift bags with brand new stuff inside like long johns, underwear, warm socks and beanies, personal hygiene items such as toothbrushes and toothpaste, and blankets or sleeping bags. It's so important to get them new stuff – nothing already used.

There is always music. Michael Murphy, a three-time Dove award winner who used to lead worship at Central, came and did worship and praise one year. At our last event, Pastor Teddy and the choir from Hope came and led us all in Christmas carols.

At Broken Chains, we save money for Christmas all year. Every dollar donated goes back into the ministry – Heather and I don't take a penny. We are serious about being good stewards of God's money. People know that. They step up and say, "Hey Cody, I heard about your Christmas thing, and I want to help."

Christmas just grew into this huge event. It's all God.

We've had challenges too. But God always uses them for His glory. And here's the thing – I refuse to beg. Just like when I lived on the streets, I won't beg. I rely on God to bring in what we need.

But it gets a little nerve-wracking sometimes.

About five years ago Christmas got pretty expensive for the ministry. It was up into the $15,000-$16,000 range. That year we were $5,000 short on being able to provide everything we needed for Christmas. We were getting really low on being able to fund the ministry, too — keep in mind that we still had outreaches to run after Christmas was over. I had no idea where we were going to come up with the money.

So I went to a Bible study and just prayed about it. I kept it to myself, didn't mention it to anyone. After the study, a man walked up to me and said, "Hey Cody, I have some clothes in my truck for you guys." So I went with him and he pulled out two big trash bags full of new clothing and gave them to me. And then he reached into his shirt pocket and pulled out a check and handed it to me. It was for $5,000 exactly.

Oh man. We were in the parking lot of the church and I shouted, "Hallelujah, thank you Jesus!" I hugged him and picked him up and twirled him around. That was cool. But there we go again: God provides. God provides.

The biggest problem we had throughout all of our big Christmas events was transportation. Every homeless person in town knew that we did these big outreaches and they knew we'd find a way to get them there. Most often, we had to go down to the homeless quarter in order to get them to the event.

We'd even been known to rent a fleet of U-Haul trucks and use them as taxicabs. This is totally against the law, I know. But. Well. Here's the story: one Christmas, Peter Blue rented us a bunch of U-Hauls because the party got so big we didn't have any way to get everybody there. I left him in charge of it.

So I was at the parking lot at Harley and the first U-Haul pulled in to drop off the homeless people. We thought there were gonna be 30 or 40 guys in the 26-foot truck and we already put blankets down for them to sit on. Well, I opened up the door, and there was like 100 people standing up inside. I couldn't believe my eyes.

A police officer pulled in right in back of the U-Haul truck with his lights flashing and he said, "Hey, who's Cody?" I said, "I'm over here. I'm Cody. Can I help you?" He said, "Man, what do you think you're doing? You can't be putting all these people in a truck like this."

I already had two undercover Metro police working the event for me in case a problem happened. One of the lieutenants walked up to the officer who pulled over the truck and said, "What's the problem here?" The officer said, "Well, these guys are putting all these homeless people in the back of a truck." The lieutenant said, " I want you to get on your radio right now and put it over the air that any U-Haul truck that is down in the homeless quarter on Christmas Day is not to be pulled over."

They both could have written us a citation. At that time, there were about 1,000 people coming. We could have got in a lot of trouble for that. Thank God we had some believers working undercover for us.

Another amazing thing is that we have never got rained on during Christmas Day. Some Christmases we'd be out there in t-shirts because the weather was so beautiful. Other times, there'd be clouds all around us and we thought it was gonna rain any minute, but it stayed dry.

For the last two years we've had to downsize the event and hold it in Justice Myron E. Leavitt and Jaycee Community Park with only a couple hundred people there – but not because of money issues; because of my health.

I was out one day hitting golf balls around with Jim, a friend of mine. All of a sudden he looked at me strangely and asked how I was feeling. I told him that I'd been feeling kinda tired lately. Jim asked what my doctor had said. I had to tell him that I hadn't been to the doctor in about three years because I no longer had health insurance.

Well Jim went home and called me later. He said, "You have insurance now." He actually bought insurance for me. So I immediately went to the doctor. I knew something was wrong, but I didn't know what.

So after a bunch of tests they found out that I was in stage 4 Hepatitis C. My viral load was like 6.5 million in my liver – the high range. My doctor immediately put me on Interferon, but it made me really, really sick. By then there was a new super drug called Harvoni. It is very expensive – $94,000 for a 90-day treatment. That's more than $1,000 a day.

Thank God Jim bought that insurance, because I couldn't have been on that. I took that treatment and was Hepatitis C free for four months, but it came back. I still struggle with it. My doctor told me that he can't do anything, but they're working on new drugs for this disease. Hopefully by the end of this year when I see him again there will be a drug that he will put me on. But I'm asking God to heal me before then.

So after I was diagnosed with Hep C and the Interferon made me so sick, we had to scale back Christmas. I just didn't have the energy ahead of time to pull it off. Although

I was too sick to preach, I wasn't too sick to go. One of our pastors preached instead and we have held it in the park over the last two years.

Part of the reason we've scaled back is that it takes three months to put Christmas together on a bigger scale and I just don't have the get-up-and-go. But hosting it in the park brings a very sweet atmosphere. We have just a couple hundred people so it's more intimate. A lot of the people who showed up before just for what they could get are gone. It's more of a Christmas party now.

Sure, I'd like to go back to having thousands of people at Christmas, and maybe we'll get to that point again. But what we are doing now is fine too.

The thing is, I'll do Christmas until my last breath because there's no better place to be but out there with hurt and broken-hearted people. They're just broken. Man, Christmas is one day you don't want to be homeless. Their hearts are feeling such pain — they're feeling such condemnation. And just that breath of fresh air, that somebody does care about them means the world to them. It really does.

Funny thing is, during the year they have no idea what date it is, except that the seasons change. But everyone knows when it's Christmas. When I was homeless, it was one of the worst days – top 10 worst days. I had bad days in front of judges and kicking drugs, but being homeless on Christmas was up there with one of the most hurtful days.

You think about your life and how you got homeless. There is such pain and agony. At that point when you face those things, there's nothing you can do about it. They all go through that. That's why on Christmas Day a lot of the homeless people are drugged up and drunk. That day is their height of pain and self-condemnation. They think about Christmases past and spending it with their families and loved ones and remember the joyful things that happened. But here they are in the midst of a storm and they can't see their way out.

That's why we're out there to tell them that there is a way out; the way to life is through Jesus. In John 14:6, Jesus Himself says, "I am the way and the truth and the life. No one comes to the Father except through me." For just a few hours every Christmas morning it's a wonderful place for us to be, out there with broken, hurting people, comforting them, hugging them, grabbing ahold of them and letting them use our shoulders to cry on. It's a good place to be.

A few weeks before Christmas, we let people at the park know that we're going to be there. We tell them to invite everyone they know. Everybody is welcome. They don't have to be a Christian. They don't have to be anything. All are welcome.

And we see God provide. We never really know how many people will show up. I'm not kidding; I've seen God multiply things so that we have enough, just like in the Bible.

For example, at the Christmas outreach we did that had 1,400 people, volunteers ran up and told me that we were running out of turkey. They said, "What're we gonna do?" I said, "I'll tell you what we're gonna do. We're gonna pray."

So I got Pastor Ray, Pastor Chris, and a bunch of other pastors who were at the event. I said, "Guys, guys! Come over here, we got to pray!" I told them we were running out of turkey. So we prayed and asked God to multiply the turkey just like Jesus did with the loaves and the fish. We said, "Lord, Lord, we need you now. We're running out of turkey. We don't have enough turkey!" There was a big line of people waiting to get their Christmas dinner.

And you know what? God multiplied it. We ended up with one of those big, huge pans left over. I'm telling the truth. We fed all the people in line and had this great big pan of turkey left. I found out later that we weren't just running low on turkey, we were OUT of turkey. Totally out of turkey.

Over the last two years when we hosted Christmas in the park, we started to run out of gift bags. We prayed that God would supply, and either everyone ended up getting a gift bag, or we had too many left over. We were running out of sleeping bags, and then all of a sudden we had more than enough. One time somebody pulled up with a truckload of sleeping bags and said, "I heard you're having an outreach." At every event over the past 10 years we've never lacked for anything. We've always had more than enough.

But Broken Chains ministry is more than a once-a-year event.

Really, we have Christmas in the park 52 weeks a year. People give us stuff all the time to take to the homeless for every outreach that we do. We have clothes, food and the Word of God.

Every day that we're out in the park is Christmas.

CHAPTER 14

Children and
Two Lunch Tuesdays

S even years ago, Hope church presented a video to the congregation about Broken Chains and what we do.

Sherrie Essy, a teacher at Del Webb Middle School in Henderson, wanted to do something to help the homeless community. She came up with an idea to provide sandwiches for our ministry one day every month. She asked her students to bring supplies from home and stay after school to make sandwiches. Now they do this twice a month.

One day I got a call from Beth Mundo from the Charlotte Hill Parent Teachers Association who wanted to meet me with a few other ladies for a cup of coffee. We met and discussed what needs Broken Chains had in order to keep ministering to the homeless. I said, "Well, number one, we could always use food."

Beth came up with Two Lunch Tuesday and it really took off. Word got around to other public schools during the first two years and we had nine or 10 schools that participated. Every month we had five teams that picked up 400-500 lunches at each school and then distributed them to the city's homeless.

The PTA has been doing it for four years now; last year there were 21 schools involved. The Student Leaders Club helps collect the lunches which consist of peanut butter and jelly, turkey sandwiches, fruit cups, chips, yogurt, drinks – whatever kids and their parents can think of. Last year we distributed 20,259 lunches. That's almost 1,000 per school.

KTNV Action 13 news station in Las Vegas did a Spotlight feature about Two Lunch Tuesday. Next year, 2016, we're looking at 30-35 schools participating in the Henderson and Las Vegas areas. We even have a school in a poorer part of town that contributes only 20 lunches but we tell them we are grateful for whatever they can do.

All of a sudden we had to come up with a creative way to distribute these lunches because five teams of people are gonna have a hard time distributing 20,000 lunches in parks. So we partnered with other programs in town and distribute through the Las Vegas Rescue Mission, Catholic charities, two Salvation Army locations, U.S. Vets, Casa De Luz, and a lot of drug halfway houses.

Sometimes the lunches go to what we call a "bean line" where the homeless people are brought in off the street for a bowl of soup and a piece of bread for dinner. On their way out the door they are given a couple of our lunches so that they have something to eat through the night and even the next morning.

I've been told that the students compete over who can bring the better lunch. That's really cool. The kids decorate the bags and write notes to put inside for a homeless person to read. Some of the schools have gone above and beyond what Two Lunch Tuesday started out to be. They do sock drives for us, hygiene bags that contain deodorant, toothbrush, toothpaste — whatever.

Another really cool thing happened this year. One of the teachers at one of the biggest schools came up with an idea. Kids aren't allowed to wear ball caps in school. So school officials sent out flyers that stated, "If you bring one dollar to donate to Broken Chains Ministry, you can wear your ball cap all day at school." I was totally blown away by this. That one school raised $600 for Broken Chains ministry.

When the homeless people find out that these lunches that we're handing them were made by children, nine times out of 10 we will see a tear running down their faces. They look at us and say, "How could a kid care about me?" I tell them, "Because God loves you, and God used that kid to make that lunch just for you." It throws them back when they think that a bunch of children got together and cared enough to go through the effort to make them something to eat. It touches them deeply.

You never could have told me that one lady seeing a video at church and taking action could have started this. That is God in action.

CHAPTER 15

Bands of Brothers and Sisters

Heather and I believe that if we call ourselves Christian and we have an abundance of something, we need to share that with somebody or with another ministry that could be in need, or somebody just starting in ministry.

Casa de Luz (House of Light) and Broken Chains started up about the same time and we partnered together early on. We were in ministry about six months and people at Casa would call us when they had something we could use; the same happened when we had extra. We work together with Bible studies and outreaches. It's funny, Casa has a saying, "Cody's really our pastor, we just loan him to Broken Chains Ministry."

But with all the rest of 'em I just get phone calls: "Hey Cody, I heard you have a homeless ministry, we'd like to help you."

Now we have a big list of sponsors that help us out with everything. There are people in the church who donate money, and corporations like Panera Bread that donates all of their bread and sweets to us one night a week. Every year Panera Bread gives us $30,000 worth of bread and sweets. I didn't solicit them – Bob Sweeney, a man from our church, originally had the account and turned it over to us.

But it's not like we just sit back and wait for people to come to us – we are proactive in getting the word out about what we do. It's just so cool to see that God provided all the sponsorship we have. And we're probably a good 75 percent funded by secular businesses.

The rest of our funding in dollars comes from Southern Nevada Baptist Association and Hope Church, and God just puts it on people's hearts to write us a check. Sometimes I get notices of payments on PayPal and I don't even know who those people are; I don't even know how they learned about us.

Everybody has a different skill or a different way in which they can help. Someone might say, "Well, I don't have any money to give." But if they open up their mind and hearts, ideas of how to help will come.

The last couple of years we got to the point where we realize that it's not enough to go to the park once a week. It's not enough to tell them, "Thanks for coming and have a good day," when someone has had an emotional moment during a sermon and repented and accepted Jesus as their Savior.

In partnering with Casa de Luz, we've started a Bible study for people who really want to get serious about learning and studying the Word of God. So we do that every Tuesday night as well as take our homeless people, whoever wants to go, to church with us on Sunday. We take them in our 15-passenger ministry bus that was donated by the Regional Transportation Commission of Southern Nevada.

Last year we helped with a Thanksgiving outreach at Casa de Luz. One of the hotels bought us 1,000 turkeys. So the people at Casa brainstormed the idea to give a complete turkey dinner with all the trimmings to whoever showed up. They could take it home and celebrate. Casa de Luz is in a really poor neighborhood called Naked City. So we gave these people turkeys and dressing and mashed potatoes and gravy and pies and cakes and all that stuff. It is a privilege and honor to be associated with all the people at Casa; Pastor Chris and his wife, Laura; Pastor Dan and his wife, Melanie; and Pastor Ray and his wife, Devon.

Riding for Jesus is a Christian motorcycle club that I belong to, and we also do outreaches. I've been a member of that for a really long time. We hosted a biker unity event in North Las Vegas where we barbequed and had music and preached the Word of God. It's taking Jesus into Donna Street where all the gangbangers are — the Crips and Bloods and all the other really violent gangs.

Missionary groups from all over the place come to help too – I think partly because it's Las Vegas. People want to change it from Sin City to Saint City. Missionary teams come out here to see what's going on in Las Vegas — Broken Chains is pretty well-known around the city. So these groups can be anywhere from young college kids in Bible school to elderly people taking a mission trip. We've had people from as far away as Africa visit our ministry.

Everybody who has come to help is very respectful. The only thing that I ask is that we have advance notice so that we can make sure we have enough food to feed them too. We will entertain any size group. The Africa team is a great example. Someone called two weeks in advance and asked if they could join us on our Wednesday outreach.

A missionary team from a Christian school in Lincoln, Nebraska visits every year, but they come to minister to Broken Chains, not to help us on the street. And that's just as needed.

Their annual visit is like a tradition – a rite of passage for freshman. My testimony is passed from class to class over the years. They come to Las Vegas for their mission trip and work us into their schedule. That's different than ministry though, because they meet us at Hope and want to spend two or three hours with me. I give them my testimony and then open myself up for questions. There are usually 20-30 students. When it's over, they put Heather and me in the middle of a circle and surround us. They put their hands on us and pray for our marriage and for our ministry, that God would bless us, protect us, and that God would show us His favor.

A lot of missionary groups from the southern states come out to help us, and the Arbor View Mormon ward here in Vegas comes out too on a regular basis. The last time they came with 30 pizzas. And you know Mormons have a ton of kids — the kids served the homeless people, it was really cool.

We have all kinds of groups like that. They're in town for a missionary trip and somehow they hear about us from one of the churches and then I get a phone call.

New City Council helps with police on board

Not everyone who works with Broken Chains donates money or food or other items or hosts outreaches. It may be hard to believe, considering where I was 10 years ago, but I was asked to work with the Mayor's Interfaith Council, and to work hand-in-hand with police on behalf of the homeless community.

I think it's funny – and a total God-thing – that the city council got a new mayor and changed their attitude toward the homeless. Instead of trying to outlaw feeding them, this new council created a faith-based group to discuss how they can help.

I got an email invitation from the mayor's assistant telling me what time they were having this meeting. I wasn't too surprised that she had my personal information because when it comes to homeless issues around Las Vegas I'm pretty well known. And there was the fact that I'd sued the city a few years earlier and won.

A lot of people are involved in the Interfaith council: from local pastors to city council, the police department, and social service agencies. We deal with six sets of problems: addictions, strengthening the family, jobs, education, homelessness and human trafficking. I'm in the homeless group. Really I should be in the addiction *and* the homeless but I chose the homeless because that's the ministry that I'm in where we deal with plenty of addiction issues.

Basically all these people from different faiths, churches and agencies come together and brainstorm about things that we can do about the city's problems, not just the homeless. For me, it's about one of my key phrases, "Not just to give them a hand out, but to give them a hand up."

The first meeting that I went to was a huge gathering with all the city officials and lots of cops. Well, it was during the summertime. Although I had on a nice shirt, it was short-sleeved and all my tattoos showed. At this meeting, I walked over to introduce myself to a group of police officers. They snuck their hands around their hips and onto the butt of their guns in the holsters like they were thinking, *Who is this guy and what is he doing here?* I introduced myself and thanked them for their service.

God put it on my heart from day one to thank the police officers for their service. This is when I really knew that God was working in my heart, because up until I got saved police were my enemies.

Now we have a really good relationship and work hand-in-hand. When my people come up missing, they help me locate them.

People ask me how I could know if someone is missing because we help so many people. This is an everyday job for me. A lot of people think that our ministry is one day a week. The actual ministry is three days a week, but the rest of the time I'm out with the guys. There are different problems that come up all of the time with the homeless. Or someone will go to church with us every week and then we can't find 'em. So I know if somebody's missing, or if somebody's been arrested; I know that because I don't see them. Now I can let the cops know; they've been a valuable tool in our ministry.

Officers have also been open about accepting insight that I can give them into the homeless mindset. They come to me for advice about how to deal with them. If I see something going on that needs their attention, I don't hesitate to call them. If they are having problems with guys that I deal with, I convey the officers' concerns to my people and say, "Hey guys, you can't be leaving messes like this because they're going to come in and arrest you all."

One of my homeless guys beat up a girl and the police were looking for him. I knew where to look — I know where these guys hang out. There have been several times where my homeless people have committed a crime and I know where they are. The police call me and tell me what they need. I have actually gone out and found who they are looking for. I'm here to help the homeless, but if they have committed a crime and I know where they're at I'll be the first one to tell the police.

The truth is that a lot of cops just don't understand the homeless issue. There is one "Ah-ha!" moment when I know that a misconception is proven wrong; I can see the officers think; *Now I get it.* I put it to them like this: "You know what? If that homeless person that you're dealing with were your son or daughter or niece or nephew, would you treat them the same way that you deal with the homeless people now?" It gives them pause. They think, *Hey, really? If that were my relative, I would not treat them the way I do these other people.*

I'm not saying that all law enforcement officers are mean — there are some wonderful police in this town, there really are.

In the areas where the police look at the homeless as a problem, I bring something to the table. A lot of them have changed their minds and realize that if it were a family member, they'd be getting them something to eat and a place to stay. What's different now is the way the officers treat the homeless, even when they've committed a crime.

As part of Broken Chains ministry, I have a printed list that I hand out to the homeless community that tells them where they can get help. A lot of officers carry copies of this list in their squad cars and hand them out. This list has feeding places, shelters to spend the night for free, feeding programs, and places where people can get temporary help like the Southern Nevada Salvation Army, Las Vegas Rescue Mission, and Straight from the Streets. There are phone numbers for places to go for teens who are in trouble and for victims of sexual abuse. The list also has hours and addresses for all the places that provide meals. You name it, a number is on there: Domestic violence. Drug and alcohol abuse. Rent and utility assistance. Everything is on that list, and the police hand out copies. It's turned into a really good relationship. In fact, when we're doing outreaches at the park and barbecuing, police officers often pull up and park just to make sure we're okay. We always send somebody over with a plate of food.

Our bond has changed to the point that I ride motorcycles for fun with some of the officers. A lot them ask me the best way to take care of problems with the homeless – like how do they get them to clean up after themselves in the encampments? They ask questions about addiction. See, the police don't know. They ask, "Where are these guys getting all this money to buy all this stuff and buy all this beer, and how do we treat them?" My answer is always, "Treat them with respect, like it was your son or daughter that you're dealing with."

Broken Chains has a great working relationship with law enforcement in Las Vegas. No one could ever have told me that would happen. It wasn't that long ago that I never would have talked to a cop. They were my enemies. Now I work hand-in-hand with them. It's really cool. I mean, only God can do these kinds of things.

CHAPTER 16

Looking for Another Cody

A lot of people who come to our ministry are in the very same shape that I was in. They are in a hard spot, their world has come crashing down, some of them are addicted to drugs, some of them are alcoholics, some of them sell their bodies, some of them are…whatever the problem is. They are the most broken, the most tormented. The "least of these," is what the Bible says.

Homeless people are broken, their self-esteem is gone, they have no hope, and they think that they'll never be normal people again. When we go to the park, when I get up to preach in front of those people, I see myself – I always remember the pain and the agony and the torment that I felt when I was in their place. I guess I'm always looking for another Cody.

When we go to the park, we treat our people with dignity. We set out a dinner that you would find as a guest in my own home. I would have no problem feeding you the same meal. Most weeks we have barbeque chicken, fruit, vegetables. Heather always has to throw in the vegetables. She's so funny; she goes around to all the homeless who are eating and says, "Now eat your vegetables, they're good for you!"

At times, groups come through who want to know more about our ministry. Sometimes they bring spaghetti or make hamburgers. One time we had a world-champion barbeque guy and he barbequed a beef brisket. Our menu switches up, but it's always a great meal.

After the meal there is a sermon and then we open the meeting up for prayer. We encourage people to come up. We let them know we are more than happy to pray with them. A lot of times we just hang out in fellowship and talk with people. We tell everyone that they're important to us — that we care what they're going through.

We also ask questions like, "Are you having any medical issues?" "Do you need to go to a doctor?" "If you're having an alcohol problem, would you be interested in going to rehab?" "If you're having a drug problem, would you be interested in going to a halfway house or rehab or a drug program?" We're there to offer them a way out of their situation.

All of us who are involved know that God uses us. We are His hands and feet. It's like Pastor Vance has said, "Either we can put it in that kitchen pot where it is contained, or we can go out and pour it out like a watering pot." Well, it is our heart to go out and pour it out.

I believe that the people I'm preaching to open up to me because I used to be in their position.

When I'm talking to people who feel all this condemnation and hurt and pain and agony – and maybe some of them have tormenting spirits — I can relate to them because I can easily take my mind back to that place when I felt like there was no hope.

That's what we're out there for — to let the unwanted know that the same Jesus who saved me will save them. Maybe God won't do the *exact* same thing for them that He did for me; and maybe he'll do something *better* for them that he did for me.

But the bottom line is, God radically transformed my life from that man that I used to be. I love this verse in II Corinthians 5:17, "For those that are in Christ the new has come."

That old Cody is gone.

CHAPTER 17

We're All They Have

B roken Chains funds provide food for the hungry and helps with immediate practical needs of the homeless community. But we also perform services that minister to basic human needs.

One way we do this is by holding Celebration of Life ceremonies for those who die homeless on the streets. Many pass away without connections to family, friends or loved ones. The police work with us and call me when one of our homeless ends up in a hospital, is dying or is found dead.

Our ministry brings value to lives who need someone to care; even when no one else knew that they took their last breath.

It's heartbreaking every time I'm called with those circumstances. It's not something you ever get used to.

We had a girl who we'd been working with a long time. Laurie was homeless and an alcoholic from during the time when I lived out on the streets. We constantly tried to get her into a program. Every time we saw her, we told her, "Laurie, Laurie, we gotta get you into a program, you're dying out here."

But she'd sit in the park and drink and wouldn't eat. We couldn't even get water into her. She'd say, "Well, if you want me to have some liquid, you should buy me a beer." She was a real tough little girl. She had a daughter and grandchildren who lived up in Alaska.

Laurie went into liver failure. Heather and I went out to the hospital to stay with her. She got so bad they moved her from the hospital into hospice. Heather and I sat with her every day. Her daughter flew down from Alaska and brought one of Laurie's grandchildren with her, but by the time they got here Laurie had slipped into a coma. Laurie was ornery as usual; it took her a couple weeks to pass.

It was so sad, because Laurie had missed a wonderful life with her daughter and grandkids. But that was just the way it was for her. Laurie's whole life here in Las Vegas was about getting drunk and prostitution and trying to get by day-to-day. That just broke our hearts, especially when we got to meet her family. I fell in love with her granddaughter; I just totally fell in love.

But the good news is that Laurie had accepted Jesus as her personal Savior years ago, even though she continued to be an alcoholic. She missed out on the abundant life that the Bible promises us. But she always let me pray with her and whenever I talked with her I got straight up into her face and said, "Laurie, you're going to die out here." And she'd say, "Well, if I die I'm going to see Jesus." That was her answer.

Laurie was like a family member to Heather and me. We worked with this girl for years. The whole thing is just so sad.

Because of our Celebration of Life Services, family members have been able to find out about their long-lost relatives. Many didn't even know they were on the streets in Las Vegas. We help to provide closure and healing for families who were disconnected from their loved ones on the streets. This also makes a statement that every life matters no matter where they sleep.

None of these people should have to die like a stray dog on the street. The police and coroner all have my ministry card. Before they even move a dead body, they call me to come and identify whoever it is. They need to run their investigation and get ahold of family members, so they need a name.

When a person from the homeless community is dying in the hospital we're there with them every day. 'Cause they don't have anybody. We're all they have. And it's our pleasure and our joy to be there and to minister to them and bring our Bibles and just be there with them. Sometimes we can get ahold of the family, but we're there with them anyway.

It's heartbreaking. We sit with them in the hospital while they're dying and pray over them. That's an honor for us: to have known them and helped them in whatever capacity we could, to be a part of their lives and to be there and pray with them when we know that at any moment they're gonna take their last breath.

We've seen a lot. As of this writing, we've had 12 people from our ministry die — and a lot of them we were close to. We consider all of them our children. It breaks our hearts.

You see it coming all along the line. That's why we're out there — to connect them to Jesus before they die without Him.

CHAPTER 18

Helping Others Break Free

Broken Chains also has an addiction intervention program. We have helped families throughout Las Vegas who need help, hope and direction.

We receive calls from people across the United States who are desperate to help a loved one; more often than not they have ended up on the streets of Las Vegas. Their families found our ministry by an online search and contacted us.

Because I lived in those trenches I know how an addict will lie to their families and others. I also know the level of accountability needed when someone is fighting the addiction of both alcohol and drugs.

In our intervention program, we help families understand the boundaries and limitations they *must* set in order to help loved ones. We also help to create accountability for those who are wrestling with substance abuse.

Our team approaches addiction intervention from the understanding that many of us have gone through the process and broken the chains of addiction through the help of God and others. We simply use our experience to help and encourage others to do the same; even when they believe that there is no hope.

When I run into somebody with a drug problem I look at different ways to help them. Because they are homeless, chances are that they don't have medical insurance because they don't have any money. There are several free places where I can place them. First, we gotta get them detoxified in West Care (Las Vegas Care), and that's a three-part program.

Depending on what I find, how addicted they are, what kind of drug they use and how often they use it, treatment can take different avenues. Some might be eligible to go to a halfway house. Some are really hardcore drug addicts that need to go into a one-year program such as the one-year free discipleship at the LA Dream Center or into the Las Vegas Rescue Mission.

Sometimes I get calls from families who want me to do an intervention.

Similar to how I decide which treatment will be best for someone, I use those steps to determine if I will do an intervention: what drug they use, how long they've used it, how addicted they are, what kind of damage it has done in the family.

From there I try to meet with the addict one-on-one. If it's a female, I require that other family members are present – for obvious reasons I will not meet with a female alone.

Once we identify how bad the addiction is, sometimes we have to do a surprise party. We invite everybody who knows that person and take them by surprise at a certain time and location. Everybody from their family and friends and people who have known them for years sits them down and confronts them with what the person's drug use has done to their own lives and how it has affected them. Then they say, "If you're ready to get help — you see this ugly guy over here with all the tattoos? He's willing to help you."

I get calls from everywhere: churches, Internet searches, referrals from others where I've done an intervention and someone got help and got clean — and the mother who ran into a friend who is struggling with drug problems. I got two interventions from when we went to Texas for a speaking engagement; their loved ones lived here in Las Vegas and were on drugs and needed help. Referrals come from all over the place.

Drug addiction is a really big problem in society. I get calls from psychologists too, once word gets around that we work with drug addicts. I have a deal with someone when it comes to counseling at the Wellness Center. Mark hates working with drug addicts and I hate doing marriage counseling. So I take all of his drug cases and he takes all of my marital counseling cases. People hear about us through their church. We've done interventions with people from all over the United States.

One of my favorite stories is about Nick. I worked with him for several years. Nick was a heroin addict. I mean he was a died-in-the-wool heroin addict. There was nothing that we could do to get him away from heroin.

Nick started using fairly young; by the time he was 19 his father walked away and got a divorce because the mom let him do drugs in the house. One day Nick's dad had enough, left, and never came back.

I worked with Nick for several years. His mom called me and I did interventions with him and tried to talk to him and get him into a program. I finally got him into the Dream Center in LA. Nick was quite a success story after doing a year there. He called and told me his plans to go to school and become a pastor because he loved working for God.

Sure enough, he came back home to Las Vegas and within his first two weeks in familiar territory started using again.

But his story gets better.

After six or seven months of doing drugs, Nick broke again. In mid-May 2013 he went back to the Dream Center. He really got it this time. He put *all* of his faith, hope and trust in Jesus Christ. When the time came that Nick was nearly ready to leave, he went into his counselor's office and begged to stay. He said, "Man, I don't wanna go back out in that world, I don't wanna be tempted by drugs, I don't want to deal with all that stuff out there. Can't you guys just please give me a job?"

Today, Nick is in charge of the intake division at the Dream Center. He's held that position for two years. It's so cool the way God works, because the Dream Center has a long waiting list to get people in. I had hookups there before

Nick, but now all I gotta do is call him and I can get some-one in real quick if I need to.

Nick was a lot of work. Getting him to this place took a lot of years. But I never gave up on him. God never gave up on him. One day Nick finally got it and he sold out for Jesus. The Dream Center now has a seminary school attached to it so he's going through that *and* running intake.

Nick's story is a huge witness to what God will do when we say, "Yes" with *all* of our hearts.

CHAPTER 19

Success Stories

My favorite part of telling people about Broken Chains ministry is the success stories. There are so many.

Rick

Rick came to our ministry in the park for quite a while. He was homeless and the way that he made his living was by riding his bicycle around town and collecting cans to turn in for cash. It's called "canning." That kept him in food.

Rick didn't use drugs and he didn't get drunk – he lost everything that he had to gambling. His addiction was strong; he'd been homeless for 12 years.

After a while, Rick accepted Jesus as His Lord and showed solid signs that he wanted to do more with his life.

Over the years I had maintained a good relationship with the guys at Impact — the rock crusher place where I had my first job when I got off the street. They needed a man to work, and I recommended Rick.

We got Rick all cleaned up, took him for the interview and they hired him. We kept in mind that Rick had a problem with gambling, though. We kept a close eye on him, especially now that he was making money and had a rent-free place to stay in a trailer just like I had.

After a month, Rick got paid on a Friday. Two days later he asked if he could borrow $100. I said, "Rick, what did you do with your paycheck?" At least he was honest and said, "I gambled it."

So Heather and I talked to his employer and worked out a system to help Rick with his money. I told him, "Okay, so here we go. Rick, it's obvious you have a problem gambling. Now, if I'm gonna work with you, here's what we're gonna do, okay? You don't have to pay rent; you have no bills coming in. Heather and I will save your money and give you $80 a week for groceries and other stuff. We'll save the rest of your money in an account for you, okay? Is that agreeable to you? Because it's not our heart to get you a job so you can put what you make into a slot machine or whatever kind of gambling it is you do. It's our heart to see you get ahead and get a little money put aside and really get on your feet and be able to buy some nice things."

Well, Rick agreed to that and we saved about $11,000 for him. He decided that he needed some transportation other than his bicycle; he wanted a scooter. At that time he had about $13,000 in his account, so I said, "Well, Rick, it's your money. If you wanna buy a scooter, let's go buy scooter." So we went and got money out of his savings and he bought a brand-new scooter. Now he's got wheels, and he's doing really good. We still get good reports from his employer.

Clark

Clark's story is similar to Rick's, except that he had a problem with methamphetamine. Like Rick, he did whatever he could to get by.

Clark started coming to the ministry in the park, accepted Jesus as his Savior, and I saw that he tried to do the right things and get off the street.

I began to trust Clark, so I asked him to work for our moving company. Broken Chains gets calls for moving jobs; the homeless men working these jobs have a reputation as expert movers. I saw that Clark was responsible with his money, so I contacted Impact and they gave him a job, too.

Seven years later, Clark is still there and working as a supervisor and heavy equipment operator with Impact. In fact, he's in charge of the whole pit that's near our church. He's doing really good.

Scott

Scott's nickname was Shaky. In fact, nobody called him by his real name. He did any kinds of drugs he could find. Whenever Scott didn't have drugs, his hands shook – that's why everyone called him Shaky. Scott would do anything to get himself high – any kind of drugs, any kind of alcohol.

Heather and I worked with this guy for a long time. He came to the ministry in the park for about seven years and he never got it.

Scott was one of those guys that when you preach and look around at the people, you can see that he's not paying attention; he couldn't care less. He's just waiting for us to serve the food.

After four years we believed that Scott was kinda hopeless. But what we have found in ministry is that if we picked out people that might be "getting it" using our own wisdom then we don't even come close to what God sees. Scott definitely wasn't on my list of somebody who's ever going to get it.

One day Scott disappeared; I heard that he'd gone back home to South Carolina.

Quite a while later my phone rang. I saw the call was from South Carolina, so I picked it up. I heard, "Hey Cody, this is Scott, do you remember me?"

I said, "Yeah…"

Scott said, "Man, I wanna tell you something brother, I am a born-again, Spirit-filled believer now!"

I said, "Scott! You gotta be kidding me."

Scott said, "No man, I go to church, I go to Bible studies, Cody. I not only have one job, I have two jobs now. I make money, I'm growing a garden, I'm doing really good."

I couldn't believe the voice that I heard on the other end of this phone was the Scott that I knew as Shaky and had decided was kinda hopeless. He was a totally different man than I had worked with for seven years.

Scott really touched my heart when he told me that when he's in church he hears my voice. When the preacher picks up a certain canon of scripture and explains it, he hears my voice explaining those same words. I can't tell you what that means to me.

Malcom

We found Malcom sleeping under a bench in 2012. He was lost, he was broken. He had very low self-esteem and was a drug addict.

I kept trying to talk him into going down to the Dream Center to get help, but he wanted no part of it. He wasn't from this earth; he was a really, really bad guy. Malcom was into a lot of crime and doing horrible things to get drugs, which included violently hurting people.

But Malcom came to the ministry in the park frequently and would say, "Pastor Cody, can you pray for me?" So I prayed for him and we talked, but I could never get him to commit to going to the Dream Center.

Well one night, two young women came from another church to help with our outreach. God led them over to Malcom. They asked him questions about his problem and why he was there. After a while, one of them came over to me and said, "Cody, can't you do anything to help this guy?"

I said, "Honey, I offer him a one-year program every time I see him." She said, "Cody, I think I have some good news for you — he just agreed to go to that one-year program."

Trying not to let my mouth hang open, I went over and talked with Malcolm. We prayed that he wouldn't change his mind and that he would stay determined to turn his life around.

In May 2015 Malcolm graduated from the Dream Center. He is now in the San Francisco Bay area working at a mission, spreading the Word of our Savior, Jesus Christ. His job at the mission is to read his Bible when people come in to get their food, and take them to the Word of God.

With his own life, Malcom shows them how God's mercy and love and grace is available to them. He took the Great Commission in Matthew 28 very seriously: "Go into the world and preach the gospel."

God sent those two women to our ministry at exactly the right time when Malcom's heart was soft enough to promise to go to the Dream Center — because I couldn't talk him into going no matter how hard I tried.

What a perfect picture of God's love, of God's grace, operating in a man's life.

Mike

When we met Mike about four years ago he was in dire circumstances. He was living in a drug halfway house, he couldn't pay his rent, he couldn't get a job, and he had lost all hope. He had given up.

Heather and I met him through the halfway house ministry. We invited him to the outreach in the park and pretty soon he started coming to church with us. Well, he got serious with God. I mean, he really got serious.

Mike read his Bible and prayed and was really into a relationship with Jesus Christ. As I started to know him, I asked what kind of work he'd done in the past. Turns out, he was an electrician. I didn't know anyone who needed one, but we prayed that he'd get a job doing that.

After that prayer, Mike had not only one job, but two jobs. He is also the official electrician for Broken Chains Ministry. Whenever we have — and we have a lot — electrical breakdowns, we call Mike.

Mike is now on his feet, has his own home, and works for a big electric company here in Las Vegas. He's a supervisor, he makes really good money and he's totally sold out for Christ.

Cathy and Ken

When I worked for UPS in 2006 we were doing a show for a company out of Florida that had just begun trade shows here in Las Vegas. Cathy and Ken were party people.

Most mornings after a night of partying hard, they came to the shows that we worked diligently to make perfect for them and were very rude to Scott and me. Both were usually hung over and wouldn't even say, "Good morning."

Scott tried on several occasions to witness the gospel of Jesus Christ to them, with no apparent effect.

On one occasion they came to town to do a show and needed help setting up. From the times they'd been around us before, they knew that I worked with a homeless ministry. So Cathy asked if I could provide 10 homeless people to help with the setup.

I went to the park and hand-selected 10 men to work the show. Of course, I was there with them while they labored. I was so proud of how hard each of them performed — and it touched Cathy and Ken deeply, too.

Later, Cathy walked up to me with tears running down her face and said, "Oh my God, Cody, these people work harder than the teamsters do. My heart has been changed about how I feel toward the homeless. They really do want to work."

That show went off perfectly. Cathy and Ken even had my guys back for the load out when the show was done.

Six months later Cathy and Ken returned to do another show where I was the carrier. I noticed that Cathy wore a cross around her neck and that they were both completely sober.

I asked Cathy about the cross. She and Ken gave their lives to Jesus. They attend church and Bible studies on a regular basis. They have three children who also got saved; they play worship music in their church band.

During that show, Cathy and Ken asked me questions about homeless ministry and how they could reproduce in Orlando what we do in Vegas. They even flew people out later to interview me about how to set up and run a ministry like ours. They now run a non-profit ministry called "A Place for Grace" in St. Cloud, Florida near Orlando.

Cathy and Ken both apologized for being so rude to us before they were saved. My reply was, "But that person is gone now; you are a new person in Christ."

Only God can do these kinds of things. You can't make it up.

Spider

Lee Strobel contacted me while he was writing his book, *The Case for Grace*. He was an atheist who set out to prove

Christianity false. Well, he ended up giving his heart to Christ and wrote a few books that most Christians know; *The Case for Christ*, *The Case for Faith*, and *The Case for a Creator*. There are many more.

Lee wanted to interview me for a chapter in his newest book. While in Las Vegas, he went to an outreach at the park with me.

At the time that Lee visited, we had this guy at the park who'd just gotten out of prison for attempted murder. His name is Spider, and he's one of the very meanest, *meanest*, I mean violent-mean guys that I've ever met – and that's saying a lot. I've met mean guys in prisons and bike gangs and stuff, but there was something extra-mean about Spider. And he was homeless in the park where we minister.

When Spider came to live in the park he just took over because he is buff and as I mentioned, really mean. He beat guys up every day. To tell you the truth, Spider was the hardest homeless man I've ever worked with. He was unreachable because he was always so high or so drunk or so enraged with his temper. He was constantly going in and out of jail for assaulting people.

One time Spider came at me and said that he was going to beat me up. I said, "Bring it on, Spider, I got some for you." Every day he was violent with somebody. Spider was really chicken the way he did it because he would cold-cock them. He snuck up behind somebody, tap them on the shoulder and plow them in the face with his fist when they turned around. That is not manly. My opinion is that you shouldn't fight at all, but if you're going to, don't do it the way Spider did it.

I spend a lot of time down at the park; I'm there every day when I drive past on my way somewhere. I always stop to make sure everybody's okay. After Spider arrived, I noticed people with black eyes or missing teeth or stitches in their faces. I'm like, "What happened to you?" They answered, "Oh, Spider hit me." I asked, "Why'd Spider hit you?" They said, "I don't know, he just got drunk and he hit me." He broke jaws, that guy. He was mean.

About a week before Lee's visit, Spider was so drunk that he fell off a curb and broke his leg. But he was determined to come to the outreach and hear the sermon on the day that Lee was there. So someone put Spider in a shopping cart with his broken leg hanging over the side and pushed him to the park.

During the middle of my sermon, I saw Lee walking over to Spider. My heart just about stopped. I had a security guard assigned to Lee because I didn't want people swamping him or doing anything. And there he was — walking over to Spider of all people. I knew that Lee's heart was changing for the homeless – we'd had a lot of conversations about the fact that they are regular people who have made mistakes — but we had 180 people at the park that night and he was going to talk to *Spider*.

Lee strolled up to Spider and said, "Hey, what's your story?"

Spider went on and on and told him all of his babble. Then Lee looked at Spider, put his arm around him and said, "Let me tell you about a friend of mine. His name is Jesus. He has radically transformed my life."

Six months later, Spider got saved. Okay? Saved!

My phone rang one day and I heard his voice on the other end. Spider said, "Cody, you're not even gonna believe me, but me and Rebecca both got saved." He was right. I didn't believe him at first. I was like, "You got to be kidding me."

Spider and his wife, Rebecca, had moved up to Washington State so he could go to work for a construction company. He wasn't drinking anymore, not doing drugs anymore — Spider wasn't violent anymore.

I caught up with Lee later at Woodlands, the church in Texas where he sometimes speaks. When I told him about Spider he almost fell over backward.

But here's the thing: all of the people that I mention — from Nick and Rick to Spider — earnestly sought God and they got rewarded. Hebrews 11:6 says, "Without faith, it is impossible to please God because anyone who comes to Him must believe that He exists, and He rewards those who earnestly seek him." They didn't seek God because they wanted something in return. They sought God because they wanted to know *Him*.

These people also found that sometimes there were people in their lives that had to go. They got to a point and had to say, "Hey, you know what? I like you but I love Him — and you gotta go." That's really what it takes, because a lot of these guys kept walking down the same road and falling into the same hole even though in their hearts they wanted to take another road.

The change in their lives boiled down to being serious with God, truly repenting and asking forgiveness. God loves prayer like that; prayers don't have to be eloquent. When you drop to your knees and get serious with God, then *bam*, stuff starts to happen.

When we find the homeless they are in disaster mode. They have been through a disaster. They don't have any hope; they don't have any way that they're ever gonna be able to work or be normal. Jesus gives us hope.

I can't take any credit. The only credit I can take in anything is being obedient to God's voice. That's what makes the difference, and that's where the magic happens. When you're determined to know Him, things happen. It is, "God, who gives life to the dead and calls into being that which does not exist." Romans 4:17.

CHAPTER 20

Six Common Questions about the Homeless and the Ministry

People don't understand how Heather and I can do all that we do and not take any money from our ministry.

The most common question we get from church people to homeless to pretty much everybody that I have a conversation with about Broken Chains Ministry is,

"How much money do you make from the ministry?"

People want to know what's really in it for us.

The short answer is: Nothing. We don't take a penny. Every cent, every dollar given to Broken Chains goes to Broken Chains. Heather and I live off of our Social Security and even tithe 10 percent of that to Broken Chains. We don't take any money.

"Cody, why didn't you go into some other kind of ministry? Why didn't you go into something where you can make a lot of money?"

Number one, I didn't choose this ministry, God did. And number two, I put it to people this way: the enemy comes to kill, steal and destroy. The enemy has these people by the throat. He's got a cocked .44 Magnum to their heads and about to pull the trigger. We're out there to snatch them out of his hand before he fires.

While Heather and I considered going into ministry, Pastor Vance warned us that we're gonna be attacked about the financial part of it. So we keep very good records. We keep track of the money that comes in all the way down to the penny; there is a spreadsheet for everything coming in and everything going out. Anybody is welcome to look at that at any time; they will see that we do not take any money from ministry.

I think that God honors that. God provides all of our needs — *all* of our needs.

When homeless people ask about it, it's with a different mindset. They can't believe that we love and care about them so much. They think that there has to be something they're not seeing, because we're out there every week bringing them more food than they can eat. They want to know if we have an ulterior motive.

Comprehending that anyone could love them is beyond them — especially those who are not believers and not even on their way to becoming one. They live at the park with nothing, so they look at us and say, "You can't tell me these guys come out and do all this stuff for free." It's just beyond them. They don't know how to handle unconditional love.

They often grasp at straws to try and prove other motives: "Well, if Cody does all this for free, why does he drive a brand-new car?" Well it's not a brand new car, it's a 2006, and our son gave it to us. "Why does Cody drive a brand-new Harley?" Well it's not a brand-new Harley, it's a 2003 Harley. I just take care of it; I bought it when I worked with UPS. They try to pick at little things because they don't want to believe that we're not getting anything material out of helping them.

What people don't know is that we don't really have any bills except electricity and household expenses. Our home and vehicles are paid for. We stretch our Social Security to make it last. God provides what we need.

The only thing that anyone could possibly pick at is that Broken Chains pays for half of our power bill at home. We have a fully-stocked pantry in our garage with two big professional freezers, a side-by-side refrigerator/freezer and a double-wide professional refrigerator that were all donated to Broken Chains. We also have an air conditioner that runs 24/7 throughout the spring, summer and fall because we store perishable food for distribution. We had to re-wire the whole garage to be able to run all the electrical stuff out there. The ministry also covers our Internet, vehicle gas/repairs and my cell phone. That's it.

It's funny, when I went to church leaders to ask advice about all this they told me I was crazy to use 100 percent of whatever money came in for the ministry — that we didn't have to go without a salary. We can legitimately take 50 percent of what the ministry brought in. But I just can't do that. It would only leave about $25,000 for Broken Chains to work with the rest of the year. So Heather and I decided that 100 percent of what comes in gets used for the Ministry.

All three of our Board of Directors are volunteers. Heather and I are volunteers. Nobody gets a salary – we don't pay anybody anything. Well, I guess there is a gray area here after all — I have a homeless guy who volunteers to set up all of my sound equipment when we do an outreach. Every once in a while I slip him a $20 bill from Broken Chains. He deserves that. Even though he lives on the street, he still does all of this work for us for free. So I'll slip him a $20 bill and I don't see anything wrong with that. He provides a service.

I believe that God honors the way that Heather and I take care of the money He gives to us; every time we've had big needs, He takes care of it. My heath issue with insurance and medication for Hepatitis C is one example. My friend has paid my health insurance for three years now.

Another example is my teeth. They were all rotten from doing drugs for all of those years. When I worked with UPS I went to Tijuana, Mexico to get them looking and feeling better and they lasted a couple years. I started having problems with my teeth again by the time we started in full-time ministry and I didn't work for UPS anymore. I went to a dentist to see what he could do and he said, "Cody, your teeth are too far gone. You need dentures. We have two options: we can give you dentures or we can do implants." I asked, "Well, how much are implants?" He said, "$35,000." And I said, "Okay. Well, how much are dentures?" He said he could do them for a couple thousand dollars. So I said, "Man, forget the implants. I can't afford that kind of money."

The dentist looked at me, then said, "Cody, wait right here." I'm not sure where he went or what he did, but I know that he's a Christian man, so I think he went into his office and prayed, because when he came back, he looked me in the eyes and said, "Cody, we're doing implants in your mouth." I thought he misunderstood me, and I reminded him that I couldn't afford $35,000. He said, "Cody, for what you do and for what you have done for this community, I want to donate implants to you. I don't want you to pay one penny."

That's God's grace. I could go on and on and on about the way He provides for us.

The bottom line is that I don't serve God for what I can get out of it. I serve God for what He can give through me. When I pray, I pray for the ministry. I pray that God's will is done in this ministry. Not Cody's will, not our Board of Director's will, not anybody's will but God's will.

"Why don't homeless people just go and get a job?"

People think that homeless people don't want to work and get out of the situation they're in.

I'll admit there are a lot of them who are comfortable with begging and not going to work and not having to pay taxes and not having to pay bills. But there are a lot of them that are willing to work, and when they're given a chance they do a good job.

As I mentioned before, we run a moving company with the ministry. I'll get a phone call, "Hey Cody, I need four guys to help me load a truck 'cause I'm moving." I provide the four guys and the customer pays them directly. Broken

Chains doesn't get a penny. All I do is set up the moves and turn it over to the guys.

A few years ago before I got too old and tired, I'd go out on the jobs with the guys. It touched my heart deeply to see how hard they worked. It literally made me cry. It just isn't true that most of them don't want to work.

We only recruit people for moving jobs that we know are clean, sober and responsible. We always follow up with a phone call: "Were these guys okay? Did they do a good job for you? Were they trustworthy? Did they take too many breaks?" But usually, before we can even make that phone call, the people call us to say how wonderful our guys were.

The guys we use are mostly now in apartments and paying their bills and have proven themselves in the ministry. They charge $20 an hour, so if they've worked a 10-hour day, that's $200. I need to know that they are not going to take that money and spend it on things I don't want Ministry money spent on.

The biggest problem with the homeless getting work is that they're homeless. That's where Broken Chains steps in. If somebody is determined to get a job, we will outfit them with new clothes, make sure their hair gets cut and whatever else it takes. The biggest thing it takes is determination and to remember that God is for you. You have to be determined that you're going to get out of your situation and that God is going to direct your steps.

It's hard for us sometimes to see people fall by the wayside and not continue with the good way that they started, but it comes with the territory.

There are a few ways that we determine if someone is serious and determined to get a job and out of their homeless situation. A good indicator is when we see them coming to ministry every week, offering to help; they're at the park on Sunday morning waiting for a ride to church, they ask, "Hey Cody, is there anything I can do to help you?" "Hey Cody, I was reading this in my Bible, I have a question about it." That transformation process is what kicks us into action.

That's when we approach them and say, "Hey, whatever you need, you let us know and we'll make it happen." We'll rent an apartment, like we did for Kim and her children, and we'll pull out all stops at that point. But we have to see determination.

Unfortunately, a lot of people we deal with are deceptive and only come to the ministry to get what they want. We need to have a discerning spirit about who is serious and who's not. We never just throw food and clothes and money anybody's way.

When someone asks us for something that involves spending Broken Chains money, we put the ball back in their court and we say, "Well, what are you doing to help yourself out of this situation?" If somebody asks me for a $65 bus pass, I ask, "Okay, so where are you gonna look for a job? How are you going to do this? Do you have identification; do you have a birth certificate?" In other words, I make sure that they're doing everything they can to get back on their feet. Only then will Broken Chains help them along financially.

Even with all of our safety measures in place, we've been burned a few times. There have been people who appear that they "got it" with all their, "Praise the Lord" and "Hallelujah" and going to church every week. We helped them with food and filled their house with furniture and helped their children and other things, only to never hear from them again. But it happens. We can't worry about getting burned all the time – once burned twice afraid is not in the Bible. It's better to get burned than to have someone go unhelped when they really needed it.

One thing we never do, outside of paying for services rendered for the Ministry, is give homeless people money. Never.

People are inventive in coming up with all kinds of emergency situations. They will say, "Cody, really, I've been out. I've applied for jobs. But now my cell phone's gonna be turned off, and I need $80 to pay the bill." In the early days of our ministry, we thought someone was serious if they'd been coming for about a month. We had a heart to help them out. So we paid the phone bill. The people disappeared. That happened with bus passes too. It happened with people who were sentenced by a judge to pay a fine – say $150 – we paid and they never came to Ministry again.

It's been a learning process all along the way. Yes, we still help people, but we put them through a little test before we start spending any Ministry money to help them out of whatever situation they're in. Nine times out of 10 the money won't go toward what they said it was for. It will get used for drugs, gambling, and prostitutes.

"What should I do when I am stopped at an intersection and there's somebody sitting there with a sign?"

Number one – don't give them money.

I would pray about it and say, "Lord, do you really want me to help this person?" If God touches your heart to help them, you could pull alongside them and say, "Hey man, are you hungry?" I wouldn't recommend putting them in the car with you — I don't care if you're a man or a woman. But if they say, "Yes," and indicate that they'll be there for a while, then go to a market and buy fruit, vegetables, peanut butter, crackers, whatever. If there's a fast food place around, buy them a hamburger or tacos or something. People can always carry bags of non-perishable food in their car. Peanut butter and crackers are always good, something with protein to put in their stomach. If people want to hand out canned food, make sure it's a pull-top – homeless people don't usually carry can openers around, or plastic spoons and forks.

Sometimes you make the effort to offer someone food and they flat out turn you away. A friend of mine was a somewhat-starving college student. He'd finished getting some groceries, put them in his car and pulled out of his parking space. As he left, he saw a guy standing there who appeared homeless and had a sign, "Will work for food."

So my friend pulled out some of the food he'd just bought and said, "Here you go, man," and the guy said, "I don't want that. I want money." Well, he didn't get any money, and he also didn't get any food. For a number of years after that, my friend never offered a single thing to a homeless person again. He was actually a bit put off by them.

That's not uncommon. The guy at the grocery store was most likely trying to get money for drugs or alcohol or something else. He wasn't after food, even though his sign said he was. One bad apple spoils the whole barrel.

Heather and I came across a homeless man walking down the road, hair all matted and just looking nasty. I pulled over to hand him a food bag. He screamed at me, "Get away from me!" I stayed calm and friendly and said, "Sir, I'm just bringing you..." "I DON'T CARE WHAT YOU'RE BRINGING ME, GET AWAY FROM ME!"

If I operated on the way that one guy reacted, I wouldn't have anything to do with the homeless. But when you run into those types of people, chances are that they are mentally ill.

"How can you tell if someone is really homeless?"

There have been exposé programs on TV and videos on YouTube where people are caught faking being homeless. They make it their job and they make a bunch of money standing off the street with a sign.

The first thing is that you can tell by their looks. The homeless will be very unkempt, unshaven, their teeth will be in bad shape, their hair will be long, and they'll normally be tan, especially in a place like Vegas — they'll have a really deep, dark tan. They'll usually be skinny and not fat.

Heather and I actually have one in our own neighborhood; we helped him out for years. There's no way this guy can be homeless because he is shaved, he wears a shirt and a tie and slacks and carries a sign, "I had a stroke, my boss fired me, I can't get work." I can't prove it, but I *know* he is not homeless. He's been out there for years on the corners around our house.

I know there are some people who make a living doing that, but I believe it's a very small percentage. Some people who are new to being homeless won't be in that bad a shape yet. The most important thing to do is pray and ask God what He wants you to do. Talk to them; ask them how they got into their situation.

Keep in mind that the homeless as a group – putting them in a nutshell — are inventive about how to get money from your pocket into theirs. They're pretty creative in doing that.

I can't emphasize it enough — wherever I speak, and whenever I'm asked — I advise: don't ever give them money. Especially if you don't know them and you don't have a relationship with them; never give them money.

Heather and I carry bags of food with us everywhere we go. They're in the motorcycle, in the van, in the Mustang. We keep peanut butter, crackers, fruit cocktail, Vienna Sausages, tuna fish, roll-up fruit things, granola bars, and bottled water. When we hand somebody a food bag, there is enough inside to last a couple of days.

"How can I provide clothing to the homeless?"

It's a good idea to carry seasonal bags. Socks are good anytime. If it is summer, clean out your closet; find shorts, thin material t-shirts, stuff like that. Throw them in the back of your car. Especially in areas where the summer months are hot – like Vegas. It only takes a couple days to get really, really smelly. Winter is a good time to get rid of your sweatshirts, jackets, jeans, rain gear - stuff like that.

Helping with clothing needs to be done seasonally. If you hand a homeless man a jacket during the summer, it's gonna get thrown in the garbage or left behind because it's not something he needs at that time.

Toiletries are another good thing to carry around. Hygiene in Ziploc bags – you could even put a roll of toilet paper in with the toothbrush and toothpaste and deodorant.

When you're out and God touches your heart to give something, just hand it out. If you can pull over, ask if you can pray for 'em. If you can't, tell them, "Here man, God bless you."

If someone really has a heart to help the homeless, I recommend finding a ministry like ours near your town or in your city and come out to volunteer. But make sure that God is the One who is calling you. It's hard work. What gets us through is knowing that it's God's Spirit working in and through us. He enables us to make a difference.

There are a lot of people who say that working with the homeless is not a good return on investment as far as effort and result. Getting the homeless to a point of salvation and productivity in society again is not a one-encounter kind of thing; it's a relationship-building process to pour the Word of God into their lives and pray and pray and pray that they "get it."

The way that we run the ministry is with the knowledge that for every life that's saved — even if only one person got saved through His ministry in us – it would be worth it to keep that one person out of Hell for eternity. God has performed miracles in our ministry.

We're not about numbers. In six years of officially working with the homeless, we've probably had 200 people that we believe really and truly gave their hearts to Jesus — who demonstrated that they got saved. Our budget is that we take in around $50,000 a year. So, we've spent about $300,000 to see 200 people saved.

But in God's economy, that's a good profit margin.

CHAPTER 21

Homelessness Can Happen to Anyone

A lot of people are just a couple of paychecks away from living on the streets. A lot of people are barely hanging on by a thread and they don't wanna think about that. For certain, there are a lot of people who are really hurting.

Sometimes we have them come to our house and get food – people we know who have good jobs and are not able to make ends meet. They can't pay their mortgage and their car payment and their insurance and everything that goes along with living – and food's always the last thing on the list, because they gotta keep a roof over their heads first.

We've come across people who worked full-time jobs and had their hours cut or their pay reduced, so we have functioned as an emergency food bank. We don't cater to people on a regular basis – we aren't set up for people to come every week and get groceries – but a lot of people are close to being homeless. Homelessness can happen to anybody

Other than carrying McDonald's food certificates, food bags, hygiene baggies, and clothing items in cars to hand out to homeless people, there are other practical ways for people to get involved and make a difference.

Wherever you are in America or around the world, use a search engine like Google and type in "homeless ministry" for your town.

Places will pop up such as rescue missions, Catholic charities, Salvation Army. Some bigger churches have programs that minister to the homeless with outreaches. If it's not listed on the website, call and ask so that they can point you in the right direction.

If I'd never worked with the homeless before but I really felt a nudging from God, I would start by volunteering with that kind of organization. It will get you out and get your hands dirty. Don't feel bad if it's not up your alley. God may be nudging you in another direction to help.

Being out with the homeless in their environment also helps you see them as people, not as a societal disease that needs to be cured.

It is worth it to get to know them. In all the years that we have been doing this, we've run into doctors, lawyers, and Indian chiefs who live on the streets. It doesn't matter where they were in life or how much they had or how much they lost. At one point, all of a sudden they're homeless. We've run into people with PhDs that are homeless. And the Indian, I wasn't kidding about Indian chiefs either, we got one right up here two blocks from us. That's not a joke.

Do I think that any of these people could have gotten out of their situation without Jesus? No.

But only God knows that answer. From my eyes, I don't think so. Because every success story that I've mentioned and all the ones that I haven't took determination to "Know Him and the power of his resurrection," like what Paul wrote in the book of Philippians.

I think that that's what makes God move – wanting to know Him. The Bible tells us that without Him, we can do nothing.

Could any of them have gotten off the streets and back on their feet successfully without Jesus? I don't know. But I do know all of the success stories in Broken Chains are because they all came into a genuine relationship with Christ.

EPILOGUE

In 2013, I got an email from Lee Strobel saying that he'd like to interview me. I'm a big fan of his. I read all of his books, *The Case for Christ* and others, and I had been to see him about three or four times. I thought his personal story was so cool — somebody who set out to prove that Jesus never existed and instead became a Christian. His whole story captivates me.

When I saw the email, I thought it was a hoax. But I emailed back, and then he said that he was coming to town in a couple of months and wanted to interview me for a chapter in his new book, *The Case for Grace*.

Well, I went running into the bedroom, yelling, "Heather! Heather! You're never gonna believe who I got an email from!" So, I wrote him back and said, "Yes, I'm up for anything that glorifies God."

We communicated a bit before he came to town and spent a couple of days together. We just had a blast. Lee came with me to an outreach at the park and he ended up ministering to Spider. Lee is such a humble, wonderful man. It was funny; when we were out in public no one guessed that he's a famous, best-selling author and speaker. He's just a regular, nice guy.

Lee interviewed me for about eight hours; my story is Chapter 6 in *The Case for Grace*.

It turns out that Lee has an arrangement with Woodlands Church in The Woodlands, Texas east of Houston where he preaches 12 times a year to give the lead pastor, Kerry Shook, a break. So Lee preaches about once a month. He had a speaking engagement coming up and wanted to preach about God's grace using my story as an example: God giving Cody Huff something that he didn't deserve, but through Cody's relationship with Jesus Christ, God's grace began to operate in his life.

So Lee invited me to come on the sly – only a few church officials knew. He did a sermon where he intertwined my story with the Bible; at the end he said, "Oh by the way, I'd like to invite a very special guest up on the stage. Cody, come on up." The whole church went nuts.

Lee asked me to share a few stories about homeless people, and asked how people can be involved, what they can do, and things that happened to me. He got a little bit into the bad parts of my story and showed mug shots too. Each of the three services that we did together was only 15 or 20 minutes.

At one point in my life I really hated to be around people and was even too nervous to go to a grocery store. But I prayed about that when I worked for UPS, and God changed me. The Woodlands has an average weekend attendance of 20,000 people – it's a very big church. But I wasn't nervous. I had already been preaching and doing speeches and sermons for different groups and it was a natural progression.

In fact, Lee brought that up ahead of time and asked how I would feel talking in front of all those people. I told him that it would be about the same as how I feel speaking at the park. I got over that a long time ago.

If I'm able to tell somebody about my Lord and Savior Jesus Christ, I'm gonna tell 'em. I'm humbled, and I'm blessed by the grace of God, that He could use a story like mine to touch so many lives. And whenever I say that sentence, I reflect back to my original prayer to God, "Lord wherever you lead, I'll follow." I couldn't have written a script better than what God has done in my life. It's been miracle after miracle. I'm a miracle. My life is a miracle. Jesus has blessed me above and beyond measure. God has never let me down. I am in need of nothing – and I mean nothing.

My friend Kenny Atcheson approached me about doing this book, and I looked at it as a chance to glorify God even more about what He has done in my life. For once, my life is not about me. It's about Him; and it's about Him turning this old man into a new creation.

My prayer going into any project is always that God will be glorified, that my story will reflect the grace of God in such a heavy-duty way; look at how this guy was before he surrendered to Jesus — look at what God has done.

My prayer is also that anybody reading my story who finds that they are on the fence about God, or maybe they're backslidden, or maybe they're going through fiery trials — that my story will rekindle their fire; that they will see that God is still doing miracles.

I also pray that people will look at less fortunate people in their community in a different light. I hope that throughout this book and the stories they read in it, that God will touch their hearts for less fortunate people instead of looking at them like they are wild dogs on the streets scrounging for something to eat. I pray that others will look at the homeless as people who have problems and need help.

When we first started in ministry, Heather and I went to a Southern Baptist convention. We discovered that for dollars spent, homeless ministries reap the least fruit out of any other ministry. It's because of the drugs, the alcohol, and the lack of commitment. We already suspected that. It's sad that a lot of churches are all about numbers and money. We determined that we would not be like that. We're about souls.

However many souls will be reached before I take my last breath is in God's hands, and all I can do is trust in Him. But until then, it's my honor and pleasure and my joy and my passion to be out with the guys, ministering to them, praying for them, helping them, to be doing anything I can. That's where my heart is. I know that a lot of people don't understand that.

At Broken Chains Ministry – the Board of Directors, Heather, me — all of us take the Great Commission very seriously. I believe that when we're doing that, God moves. When we're out there and ministering it's not only about feeding their bodies. My heartfelt prayer and wish is that all of those people would be hungrier for the Word of God than they are for that chicken sizzling away on the barbeque.

I hope that we will come to a place in ministry where everybody would show up with their Bibles and their pens and notepads and just hang on every word that is preached, so that we could *all* go a little deeper into the Word of God.

And that's the way I feel.

Cody Huff

How You Can Help

Easiest ways to help

1. Be nice to the homeless. They are people too. Some are homeless following a tragedy or something that is no fault of their own. Thousands of people in our country are two paychecks away from being homeless; it can happen to anyone. Others have become homeless due to addictions and poor decisions. Although they are responsible for their situation, they should not have to suffer forever. We like to say, "We give them a hand up and not a hand out."

2. Post our Amazon link to this book on your Facebook or Twitter page.

3. Write a book review on Amazon.

4. Pray for people who are less fortunate.

More easy ways that you can help

5. Keep food bags or clothing in your vehicle to give away when the opportunity is in front of you. After this section you will find a tear sheet of items.

6. Give copies of this book as a gift to friends and family members. This helps the homeless through our ministry, but it may also help the recipient because they will learn more about the homeless plight.

7. Come to our ministry in the park and have some bar-beque. As I stated earlier in the book, we make quality meals that we would serve to guests in our home; you are welcome to join us in Las Vegas.

8. If you go to church, share a copy of this book with your Pastors. It may give them ideas about how to effectively help the homeless. It may lead to an invitation from your church for me to speak about homelessness. I would be honored to shake your hand in person while we raise awareness for these forgotten and misunderstood people.

9. If you know a police officer, give them a copy of this book or share the chapter where I wrote about working with the police in effectively dealing with the homeless issue.

10. Send a copy of this book to your state Governor with a note stating, "This group knows how to help the homeless. Please contact them for assistance in doing something about the homeless in our state." Or make a donation equal to the price of this book plus shipping and we will send a book to your state Governor in your name. Include your name and state with your book donation. We will look up your Governor's name and address and send a book on your behalf.

You are a Rock Star for the homeless

11. Google "homeless ministry" and find those in your area. If there is one that you would like to help, great.

12. Visit our website and invest in the homeless. Our website is **www.VegasBrokenChains.org**

Tear-away supply page

Donations to homeless ministries or to carry in vehicle

- Men's white crew socks (size 6–12)

- Ladies/Men's shirts (medium and large) – weather appropriate

- Ladies/Men's shorts in summer

- Ladies/Men's sweatshirts, jackets, warm pants in winter

- Single serving pop-top cans of pork & beans, chili, tuna, Vienna sausages, snacks

- Single servings of fruit

- Small jars of jam, jelly, peanut butter

- Single serving drinks

- Plastic silverware (can be bought in packages that contain silverware, napkin and salt and pepper)

- Travel size toiletries – shampoo, lotion, deodorant, toothpaste, toothbrushes, Chapstick, razors

- Saltine or Ritz crackers

- Bottles of water

- New Testament Bibles (lightweight)

Broken Chains Ministry Business Partners and Sponsors

Broken Chains Ministry is supported by past and present business partners and sponsors in our community and around the world. The positive impact that these leaders have made for the homeless in our city will never be forgotten. We could not operate without their charitable contributions both financially and with material goods.

Hope Church, Las Vegas, NV

Pastoral staff and members provide consistent financial support and leftover food donations from church events.

www.HopeChurchOnline.com

Lee Strobel

His latest book, *The Case for Grace*, (February 2015) includes a chapter with Pastor Cody's testimony. Lee came to Las Vegas in 2013, attended a weekly outreach in the park and spent an entire day interviewing Pastor Cody. Lee has also donated several copies of his book to Broken Chains to help raise money for our ministry. To find out how you can purchase Lee's book and help Broken Chains Ministry with your purchase, go to www.vegasbrokenchains.org/where-youve-seen-us/ and click on the book, *The Case for Grace.*

www.LeeStrobel.com

Panera Bread Local Store #4080, Las Vegas, NV

Panera Bread provides Broken Chains Ministry with a weekly dose of goodies from bread to cookies and yummy pastries. They also donate a majority of the handouts that are delivered to the homeless and needy at our weekly Wednesday night outreaches.

www.PaneraBread.com

Las Vegas Harley-Davidson, Las Vegas, NV

The managers at Las Vegas Harley-Davidson consistently donate financially to our ministry. Throughout the year this business hosts in-store food, water, and clothing drives for our ministry as needs occur. When we send out occasional quick updates with current items needed, this store is always one of the first to respond and provide support for those specific needs.

www.LasVegasHarleyDavidson.com

St. Rose Hospitals of Southern Nevada, Henderson and Las Vegas, NV

The St. Rose network of hospitals donates bottled water whenever we need it. They actually make it a competition between all three of their Las Vegas hospitals as to who can donate the most. At one time they donated more than 1,000 cases. This comes in handy for our ministry during the summer to hydrate the homeless because of the high temperatures in Las Vegas.

www.DignityHealth.org/Las-Vegas

Cube Smart Storage, Henderson and Las Vegas, NV

Cube Smart provides Broken Chains with a discounted rate on storage for all of the donations that we acquire and distribute to the homeless throughout the year. While their partnership is not visible to many, what they provide helps to ensure that the helping hands of our ministry have donations to give when needed.

www.CubeSmart.com

Regional Transit Commission of Southern Nevada

In 2013, RTC donated a 16-passenger bus with a wheelchair lift. The bus has become a valuable tool for our ministry. From donation pick-ups for our Two Lunch Tuesday program, to ministry events, even taking homeless to various appointments including hospital, doctors, Bible studies and church on Sundays, this donation is a valuable resource for our ministry.

www.rtcsnv.com

Tiers of Joy Wedding Cakes, Las Vegas, NV

Tiers of Joy is run by a compassionate, caring woman who donates food to our ministry throughout the year. When the business owner found out that we had a need for keeping perishable food, she stepped up and donated an industrial refrigerator and freezer. The food portion of our Wednesday night outreach could not happen without Tiers of Joy's donation that prevents food from spoiling during our hot summers.

www.TiersofJoyLV.com

Evident Productions, Las Vegas, NV

Evident Productions financially supports Broken Chains Ministry throughout the year. They have also coordinated logistics for transportation and tables and chairs for our large Christmas outreaches.

www.EvidentProductions.com

Southern Nevada Baptist Association

Quarterly financial support

www.snba.net

Las Vegas Rescue Mission

Has donated 75 percent of our food needs since we started in ministry six years ago.

www.VegasRescue.org

Casa de Luz

Our sister ministry: we support each other; we do bible studies and events together.

CasadeLuzLasVegas.org

Riding with Jesus

A sister ministry: we join forces in all local biker events.

www.RidingWithJesusmc.org

Arbor View Church

Members donate food and clothing and serve at several of our outreaches each year.

Food Pros

Each week, they donate snacks and chips.

Creative Profit Pros

They are completely responsible for the creation and publication of *Handcuffs to Broken Chains*.

www.CreativeProfitPros.com

To find out more about having Cody Huff as a speaker at any event, how you can donate items to Broken Chains Ministry, to donate online, or if you are interested in becoming a partner or sponsor, contact him at www.VegasBrokenChains.org

49306856R00119

Made in the USA
San Bernardino, CA
19 May 2017